DO LOVE

A Love Hack's Path to Spiritual Maturity

Andrew Rankin

WestBow
PRESS
A DIVISION OF THOMAS NELSON

WestBow Press books may be ordered through booksellers or by contacting:
WestBow Press
A Division of Thomas Nelson
1663 Liberty Drive
Bloomington, IN 47403
www.westbowpress.com
1-(866) 928-1240

Author photo by Leslie Everett, LE Portraits
Cover image by Douglas Henderson

ISBN: 978-1-4497-8702-8 (sc)
ISBN: 978-1-4497-8701-1 (hc)
ISBN: 978-1-4497-8703-5 (e)

Library of Congress Control Number: 2013904032

Printed in the United States of America
WestBow Press rev. date: 3/12/2013

DEDICATED TO

Laurie,
my bride
and partner in love,

and Freedom Church,
the Bride of Christ
and fellowship of love hacks.

"Little children, let us not love [merely] in theory *or* in speech but in deed and in truth (in practice and in sincerity)."
1 John 3:18 (AMP)

TABLE OF CONTENTS

INTRODUCTION

"Love never fails," so the Bible tells us. This is true of God's love but not of ours. Our experiences of love, whether given or received, are marred with failures and shortcomings. We crave what we cannot seem to give or get. Somewhere in our internal world, love gets tangled and distorted with our mixed motives, ever-changing feelings, wavering intentions, and misinterpreted actions. Love may not fail, but we have failed at love.

You would think that for something so common to the human experience and so universally desirable, we would have a crystal clear understanding of the meaning and expression of love. But people are notoriously vague and clueless about it. Love's meaning is elusive ... as is its reality in our everyday lives. I have loved enough to know that I do not love well. My goal is not for you to love like me, rather to point toward the greatest lover of people the world has ever known—Jesus Christ.

This book is not a book on marriage or romantic love. It's not specifically about family dynamics or solely about justice and benevolence. It relates directly to all, but is intentionally designed for broader applications. Love is to be done in *all* our relationships, not only with a narrow band of people we call family or to a specific church group or friendship clique. Love is to be our comprehensive way of life because we follow Christ. We need an understanding of love that is applicable to all human relationships—a baseline definition and a way of acting that works in real life.

Even as Christians, we give lip service and airtime to love, but we haven't given it much biblical study, serious thought, or world-changing application. We've been so immersed in a culture that equates love with feelings and matters of God with subjectivity that we hardly know if we ever really love God and others at all. We need to discover what love is, where it comes from, and how to actually do it. Until we ourselves are transformed by God's love into people who do love, we will never fulfill the Great Commandment to love God and others.

Love's greatest expression is found in the oft-quoted John 3:16, "For God so loved the world, that he gave his one and only Son." God *is* love, so He relates to us in love. His best and clearest expression of love is His Son, Jesus Christ. Love is given or bestowed upon the beloved. Love's nature is to give, not take. And giving, however expressed, is always an action. It's tangible and real. Sentimental or romantic love has meaning only as it is expressed, whether verbally or by action. Thoughtful words or a love song become love when shared or sung. Being deeply moved with compassion for the poor, hungry, and vulnerable is good only if it includes being moved to action. Justice and compassion need action to become a force for change in society.

When we put the incarnation of God in Christ together with love expressed tangibly through words and actions, we arrive at incarnational love.[1] It is this love that Christ commands us to do. With our very physical and hectic human lives in this chaotic real world we are commissioned to love through the giving of our lives away through actions and words that will benefit and bless others.

In this book I have included short chapter breaks called "Confessions of a Love Hack." This began as a fun and lighthearted way to point out my own ineptitudes as a loving person. As more of these experiences emerged from my memories, I became aware of how much of a love hack I really am. These stories will hopefully help you understand those moments in your own life where love comes up short. Until we come to terms with our inability to love others as Christ loves them, His love won't be fully matured in us. It is the awareness of our unlove that helps us look to Jesus for inspiration and empowerment.

Be aware that I often use the word *unlove*. This is intentional as unlove is understood as being broader than hate. Hate is but one piece of the unlove pie. When John tells us that "whoever does not love abides in death,"[2] he deliberately steers clear of the word hate. The lack of hate does not guarantee that love is given. Unlove includes all attitudes, words, and actions that are not loving. For love to be Christlike, it must go beyond merely doing no harm. Love must actively and deliberately do good.

Love is too vast of a subject to be exhausted in a single volume ... or even in a library of books. This book will have gaps in it. Some of these are known and intentional; others are unknown and unintentional. I do not claim to have plumbed the depths of every aspect of love, but only to have thought long and hard about it in light of Christ, the Bible, and my failures. I am merely one voice among thousands who have uttered words on a topic that we can only know in part. I long for the day when we will know love fully (1 Cor. 13:8–13).

I openly confess that I am a love hack and do not claim to have attained a life characterized by love. I have experimented with loving others, and have even started to intentionally work it into my life's rhythm. The terrifying thing about writing a book on the inexhaustible subject of love is that I will inevitably disappoint others who look to my insights and example. I know that my head and my heart have a gaping love hole in them. If you want perfection in love, you must look beyond me to Jesus.

The foundation for this book is simply this: If love is to be love at all, it must be Christlike. The very epitome of Christ's sacrificial love is its incarnational nature. He did not merely teach on love, He *embodied* it. Real love is expressed through a human life in this reality called planet earth. Love is as tangible as Christ's physical body, spoken words, and visible actions. Anything else is just love theory.

"By this we know love, that he laid down his life for us, and we ought to lay down our lives for the brothers" (1 John 3:16).

CHAPTER 1

Love Hack

"Pursue love."
1 Corinthians 14:1

"Love alone is credible."
Von Balthasar's Credo

"Love doesn't sound so dangerous until you've tried it."
Paul Wadell

I am a love hack. I have not loved well.

I am a love theorist, but an inconsistent practitioner.

I follow One who teaches me to love, and that's the problem. I'm not a very good student. My progress is slow. Sometimes I regress.

I'm seriously love-challenged. When the love gene was being passed down, it either skipped me or mutated horribly. Somewhere in life, I, like Dr. Seuss's Grinch, seemed to receive a heart that was "two sizes too small." If love were a bank account, the bank would have closed mine for failure to maintain a minimum balance.

The confusing part is that the rest of me seems to be satisfactory enough. My brain seems to work just fine. I've earned advanced degrees academically and appear intellectually challenged only to my teenage sons. My will seems adequate. I can make and follow through with decisions. I am fairly disciplined with my time, money, and life. My body is still holding up decently for a middle-aged guy. I hold a black belt in karate and exercise often. Socially, I get along well with others. But unfortunately, my heart is just not as healthy or sane as the rest of me.

It's like I have CCFS—Chronic Compassion Fatigue Syndrome. I can't lift any love weights or run any love laps. I cannot count the times my wife has been utterly baffled by my inability to love. My speechless, glazed stares apparently are a dead giveaway to my hollow soul.

Love is a foreign language to me. I hear the words all around me, but my capacity to grasp the obvious is stunted. My love machine has faulty wiring. Jesus' new command to "love one another" always seems new to me—new as if I'm unaccustomed to it. It's as if I'm learning to walk all over again, like a baby taking its first stumbling and faltering steps. The love walk is awkwardly unfamiliar to me. I find myself hitting coffee tables and frequently falling on hard concrete rather than really making forward progress. I prefer to lie on my back, drool on colorful teething toys, and leave the real loving to the adults.

But even as I write these things about myself, I recognize that I am making my unlove seem cute and harmless. Truth be told, my marriage has suffered deeply because of my inability to express love tangibly to my wife. My lack of love has not been the source of laughs and smiles, but sadness, anger, and deep heartache. I have had to hear and accept the reality of the words: "You think you love me better than you do."

When my love is questioned, I return fire quite defensively. How dare anyone question the existence or effectiveness of my love? I know that I intend to love, that in my mind my love is faithful, committed, and true. My motivations to love my wife, kids, and friends are genuine. But this is exactly what God exposed to me. I am a great lover of people ... in my own mind ... in my own dreams ... in my own world. However fantastic my loving motives may be, until I can convert them into loving actions, no one benefits.

We've all heard the sentiment, "It's the thought that counts." Not true. There's a huge difference between thinking about buying flowers for a wedding anniversary and actually buying the flowers. Trust me; I've found this out the hard way. The thought of attending a child's piano recital or soccer game isn't the same as sitting there in the front row and cheering them on. A grieving widow doesn't experience your love theory, only your loving presence and comforting words. The hungry person at a homeless shelter can't quite sink his teeth into your good intentions like he can some meatloaf and mashed potatoes. We don't act without thoughts, but thoughts alone don't "do" anything. We do not express genuine love until we take specific actions. The road to hell is truly paved with good intentions that never morph into action.

The awakening required to rouse me out of my self-delusion was painful. To admit that I was knowledge-fat and action-thin meant that my faith was worse than anemic: it was on life support. In the words of Paul, "I am nothing … I gain nothing."[1] *My* love was *nothing*. My love lacked the heart and actions of Christ. My "love" was actually "unlove." Unlove is not life-giving. Unlove has slowly bled the joy out of my marriage and my wife. God's timing for waking me up with these fresh downloads on love could not be more timely or significant. It's not what I expected or even wanted, but it appears to be the medicine that my sick soul needs.

For these reasons, I believe that I am one of the least likely candidates to write a book about love. Isn't this like asking a tree stump to explain the finer nuances of quantum physics? Nonetheless, I'm asking you to walk with me on this journey of discovering and living out Christ's love. God is changing my life as I learn to love as Christ loves. Joy has been rekindled in my marriage and life. I find fresh strength to extend myself to others. As you learn how to love more deeply, I believe that your life will morph into a more Christlike one as well.

We Are Love Hacks

The truth is that we are all love hacks. Ask yourself some questions: Have you intended to do something loving, but failed to follow through? Have you expected something, however small, in return for love? Have you, with the best of motives, done what you thought was loving only to find out later that it wasn't the right action at the right time … and that you instead came across as insensitive, condescending, or manipulative? Have you tried to say loving, healing words only to find that what you said actually further perpetuated a relational rift? We live with our grand delusion that we give more than we take, that our intentions are nobler than they are, and that our actions are more loving than they actually appear.

Still not convinced? Think about your last forty-eight hours in light of

Paul's simple definition of love in 1 Corinthians 13:4, "Love is patient, love is kind." When someone slowed you down in traffic, the checkout line, or by turning in a late report, did you respond in a patient and kind way? When your husband, wife, or kids made you late to an appointment, did your attitude or actions convey your long-suffering patience and compassion or something much darker?

Too often we convince ourselves, even if secretly, that we are not love hacks. We believe that our love is pure … until we compare it with the love of Jesus Christ. The simple words of Jesus set the love bar high: "love one another as I have loved you."[2] It's the "as I have loved you" part that complicates our scenarios and implicates us all. If we only had to love one another as we deem fit or as we believe the other person deserves, we could find a loophole in the command. What Jesus Christ does skillfully with a scalpel, we love hacks do with a machete. Our results speak for themselves. We unavoidably butcher relationships and mangle people. It's not that we are intentionally mean, but our attitudes and actions are crude and barbaric. Alas, to love as Christ loved us is the standard from which we all fall painfully and pitifully short.

Unlove is the disease that afflicts us all. If our physical bodies reflected the true condition of our love, we would be shocked at the sight. We would rush immediately to the local ER and demand medical attention. When it comes to love, no one is self-contained and self-sufficient enough to be immune from the damages of unlove. Unlove is *the* human epidemic that creates more casualties than any war, famine, or disease. The two common denominators for humanity are our inner awareness that love is the highest good and the reality that we all inevitably live as love hacks.

Hope for Love Hacks

Is there hope for hacks like you and me to learn how to love? I can confidently say yes. Examples abound in the New Testament, but let me share two of them with you.

The apostle John is referred to often as the apostle of love. He often referred to himself as "the one that Jesus loved," and love dominates his letters. John's gospel includes the new commandment of Jesus to "love one another as I have loved you." Of all the apostles, we associate love most with John. Yet, as a young man, John was a love hack. His nickname as a "son of Thunder" clues us in to his love deficiencies. Is compassion the defining trait of a man who wanted to call fire down on the Samaritans for their inhospitality to Jesus and His disciples?[3] Is sacrificial love the picture you see when John and his brother James selfishly asked Jesus for the best seats in the future kingdom of God?[4] Yet the experience of the death and resurrection of Jesus transformed John into becoming the apostle who championed love as the gold standard of the Christian life.[5] If John could become loving, then you and I can as well.

The apostle Paul penned the famous "love chapter" in 1 Corinthians 13. In fact, Paul mentioned love in every one of his letters. The change between the pre-Christian Saul and the converted Paul was dramatic, permanent, and can only be explained as a head-on collision with God's grace. Paul went from being a love hack who persecuted, arrested, and even killed people associated with Christ to a man whose tangible and sacrificial love for God and others was legendary. Paul knew that if God could transform his sin-hardened heart into the grace-softened heart of a lover, God could do the same for anyone.[6]

Is there hope for us love hacks? Yes. The same grace and love that changed the apostles is the same grace and love offered to us.

I have not reached full maturity in my love, but it is the path on which God has placed me. For now, I am a rat in God's laboratory of love. His purpose is to change me into the loving image of His Son, Jesus Christ. God methodically uses all of my relationships and life experiences to this end. As I run the maze and find the dead ends of my unlove, God redirects me once again to simply follow Jesus. If you are willing, God will take you along for this same life-changing journey. All of us love hacks are invited into His lab to be transformed into lovers of God and others.

The Love Flywheel

What is love? How do I get it? How is it to be given or expressed? The answer to these questions, if applied, will transform your life and literally change the world. But as a love hack that's been in the love lab for several years, this may sound easy enough until you actually try to love others. Love hacks need to find the value of the love flywheel.

A flywheel is a mechanical system that relies on the power of momentum to provide a steady flow of energy. For example, on playgrounds you may find a merry-go-round. This isn't the kind that is motor-powered at the county fair, but the simplest form that requires human power. As a kid, I remember my friends and I crawling on the merry-go-round at the local park while my dad stood beside it and pulled and pushed until we were spinning so fast that we were terrified to jump off, and then when it finally stopped, we were too dizzy to walk. The ride started off slowly as my dad got the merry-go-round initially moving. The first few rotations were slow but consistent accelerations. Once my dad got the contraption spinning, the weight of the merry-go-round combined with the weight of the kids gave it the inertia to spin powerfully. Once the merry-go-round reached cruising speed, it required much less effort to maintain.

When it comes to love, there are four stages on the love flywheel that we need to experience. These four stages need to be repeated throughout our lives for us to maintain a consistent life of loving God and others. This flywheel may seem slow and clumsy at first, but remember that you are simply going through the right motions that build momentum. As you learn to walk in the way of love, you will love more quickly and purely. If you disengage from God in this process, you will eventually grind to a halt and love will be laborious and burdensome, if it exists at all.

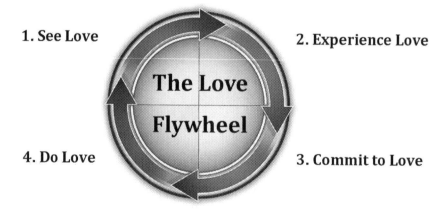

1. See Love **2. Experience Love**

The Love Flywheel

4. Do Love **3. Commit to Love**

1. See Love. Until we understand that love is the most important path of life, and truly value and seek its desirable results, we will do little about it. Although there may be numerous examples of love we can look to for inspiration, there is none greater than that of Jesus Christ. Yet even Jesus looked to His heavenly Father for His vision of love. Jesus said that He only does "what He sees the Father doing."[7] Jesus saw God loving Him and the world, so He in turn loved the Father and the world. The best way to "see love" is to study the life and death of Jesus Christ in the New Testament. From a biblical standpoint, Jesus' death on the cross is the pinnacle of love and defines all other loves.[8]

On the love flywheel, this is the beginning stage where you first understand that it would be beneficial to be loved and to learn how to love others. You first see love clearly in Jesus through His example of love and selfless sacrifice. You may also find inspiration from others who have learned the love way of Jesus—people like Mother Theresa, your parents, or just a loving friend or church leader. This stage will be covered fully in chapters three and four.

2. Experience Love. Until you personally experience the love of God in Christ, your understanding of love will be humanistic and limited. There are no shortcuts here, and an experience of God's love cannot be manufactured or coerced. The movement from intellectually acknowledging Jesus as the loving God-man in the Gospels to wholeheartedly embracing His love is mysterious and life-changing. This step is intensely personal and absolutely necessary.

Personalizing God's love comes as you respond positively to His invitation to receive His love. Many people are reluctant to say *yes* here because they feel unworthy and undeserving of His love. A *no* to His clear *yes* is not God's rejection of you, but your rejection of God. One's first experience of love always comes as a gift—never as an obligation to receive it or reciprocate. As we simply receive God's love and enjoy it, we open an internal door in our hearts that makes all other loves possible and powerful.

As far as the flywheel of love goes, it is precisely here that the energy of God is transferred over to us. As we know and experience God's love, it empowers us to love others. Without this initial experience, our love flywheel will not spin. Without God's love being repeatedly experienced, the love flywheel loses momentum. This stage will be addressed in chapter five. The power to love God and others is directly connected to our experience and acceptance of God's love in Christ Jesus.

3. Commit to Love. We must want to love. By want, I don't mean "wish." We must genuinely want to love as Jesus loves. We must be determined and resolved; we must choose love and will it. This transfers the power of God's love into our realm. This commitment means that when opportunities arise for us to express love, we will love. We live now with a predisposition to love.

When a couple exchanges marriage vows at their wedding ceremony, they have not yet expressed love in the real trenches of married life. They have confessed a lifetime of commitment to love, but they have not done the things that love will require of them. Their "I do" means they *intend to* love, cherish, and be faithful to the other. This step is important, but love's test is not when everyone is dressed up, cooperating nicely, and flush with the intensity of the moment. Love's real test is in the circumstances of daily life where intentions are converted into loving actions. Without a solid "I do" of commitment, subsequent loving actions will not materialize into "I did."

Many, many people at this commitment stage believe that they are loving God and others. They are well poised to love, but they haven't *done* love. Seeing and receiving love from God fills us up with love. Commitment to love others is an inward decision to love others, but it is not the tangible acts of love itself. The "I do" to loving God and others has been made. Now it's time to move into loving actions … the difficult part. This stage is covered in chapter six.

4. Do Love. The fourth stage on the love flywheel is where we actually do something loving. It is a tangible action that actually benefits someone else. This is the crucial moment when what's been going on inside of us becomes expressed in a way that benefits others. The phrase "do love" is literally that—an action, a behavior that is expressed. This is how love moves from our inner, private life into the outer, public world. While our initial acts of love may seem small, over time we build the momentum of loving others consistently and even unconsciously. We make a difference in the world when we actually do love. This stage is discussed in chapters seven through ten.

These four stages are not linear, but circular. You never mature beyond the need to constantly see and experience the love of Jesus. We must go back to Him often to keep our love fresh. This is how our hearts are continually renourished by the love of Christ so that we can give and give and give love away without depletion. This simple understanding of the love flywheel reflects reality, and we will discover these truths as we move forward.

Think of it this way, the child on the merry-go-round isn't traveling anywhere new; she is simply following a well-ordered, familiar path with increasing speed and momentum. As we follow the love flywheel of Jesus, this path will be continuously traveled with increasing maturity and effectiveness in the love way of Jesus.

Even love hacks can learn how to love.

CONFESSION OF A LOVE HACK

Kings vs. Queens

I do not vacation well. I have the dreaded hurry sickness.

Spending downtime with people moving at a pace far slower than mine is hell to me. And, consequently, I turn my inner hell loose on others. I prefer (read "demand") high-energy activities to sitting around idly watching the grass grow. In matters of love, I am ADHD. Unlove is impatient and curt.

I could pick almost any one of my vacation as a shining example of being a love hack, but a recent one will suffice. One summer, my family met with my parents in a cabin in the mountains of New Mexico. The weather was beautiful, the air was cool, the scenery gorgeous. We hiked, fly-fished, played tennis, threw Frisbees, shopped Santa Fe, and generally had fun.

One evening, my son Jonathan and I challenged my wife and mother to a game of Spades. The "Kings" were serious card sharks. Jonathan played semi-pro Spades in his college dorm weekly; I played frequently online. Our combined career wins and skills were daunting. The "Queens" were clearly out of their league. My seventy-four-year-old mother didn't even know how to play the game. Jonathan and I were salivating over a quick, painless victory so that we could move on to the next "fun thing."

The game was neither quick nor painless.

I was used to virtual Spades, where my online competitors either played quickly at expert level or were mercilessly replaced. I had no time for incompetent, slow gamers. Playing cards in real time with a real person who didn't understand the rules or strategy was enormously taxing. As the game proceeded, I became increasingly irritated at the waste of time or the lack of mental focus. I did not act in love to ones that I love. I was more concerned with the pace of an insignificant card game than for the most significant people around me.

I lost. Twice.

The Queens outloved us and outscored us. Ironically, it was their victory that exposed my heart. Even when I'm "relaxing," I'm a love hack.

Dear God, save my family from me. Save me from the hurry sickness.

CHAPTER 2

Love Sick

"Hear the word of the Lord, you Israelites,
because the Lord has a charge to bring against you who live in the land:
There is no faithfulness, no love, no acknowledgement of God in the land."
Hosea 4:1 (NIV)

"There can only be two basic loves:
the love of God unto the forgetfulness of self,
or the love of self unto the forgetfulness and denial of God."
St. Augustine

"Life is to love and to be loved."
Mother Theresa

*L*ove: the subject of more songs; the cause of more heartaches; more desired than a buried treasure; hoarded like a limited commodity.

Such a simple word with profound meaning—it's so profound we're left speechless, as in not really sure what to say about it other than it's a good idea. Love expert Gary Chapman says that "Love is the most important word in the English language—and the most confusing."[1] We know love is important *and* we don't understand it. We're left with a gaping hole in both our hearts and heads. Welcome to the human race; we're all love hacks.

Let's face it: we just don't "get" love. We're love sick. It's not so much that we're sick of love, but our version of love is unhealthy and anemic. Love is certainly confusing because of its complexity. It's layered and nuanced, just ask any person who's married with children. The love that drew the couple together may be romantic and reciprocal; the love that the mother has for her child may be maternal and only partially reciprocal. The love for friends and coworkers is of a different degree as well.

It's hard to imagine that the word "love" is even capable of carrying all the different meanings associated with it ... not to mention every day loves from "I love ice cream, the Packers, classic rock, and hot coffee." We have puppy love, free love, and tough love. We use this word for flippant farewells and our most soul-wrenching prayers. We've spread the word love on just about anyone and everything.

One of my favorite pastimes in recent months is to ask people randomly to define love. I'll usually say something like, "I'm doing some research on love. Can you help me define love? I'm not talking about romantic love, but love in general—simply a short definition that would apply to a couple, a parent–child relationship, or just between friends." Their initial reaction is that of bright eyes and eagerness, because *everyone* thinks that they know about love. Their second reaction is that of a furrowed brow and stammering phrases. People think they know love until they have to define it or explain it. Then the confusion really begins. Answers vary:

- "It's a warm feeling of compassion."
- "Being nice to someone."
- "A mysterious cloud of energy."
- "A chemical state of mind influenced by genetics and environment."
- "Something you have for people you like."
- "A feeling of connection between two people."

You would think that people would know exactly what love is. But, as seen from a sampling of responses to "what is love?" people are notoriously vague and clueless. Love remains one of the least understood or contemplated virtues. While I know that I do not comprehensively understand love, much less practice it as well as I should, I do want all people—Christian or not—to take a serious look at this highly praised, but imperfectly practiced thing called love.

The Importance of Love

Love is an important word, and not just because Chapman says so. Our understanding of love will affect virtually every aspect of our lives. In this regard, love ranks up there with God, Jesus, and the Holy Spirit. Why? Because the Bible says that "God *is* love."[2] It's not just that God loves us or that He does loving things, but that He *is* love. Love is a profound part of His nature. If we mess up our definition of love, we've just messed up our definition of God. Understanding love is as high stakes as it gets.

When asked what the greatest commandment is, Jesus repeatedly answered:

> "The most important is, 'Hear, O Israel: The Lord our God, the Lord is one. And you shall love the Lord your God with all your heart and with all your soul and with all your mind and with all your strength.' The second is this: 'You shall love your neighbor as yourself.' There is no other commandment greater than these." (Mark 12:29a–31)[3]

In Matthew's gospel, He includes, "On these two commandments depend all the Law and the Prophets."[4] In Luke's gospel, Jesus adds, "Do this, and you will live."[5] To love is to do what Christ considers most important. To love is to live.

Of all the commandments Jesus could have chosen as well as all the verbs He could have picked, He opted for love. So many other worthy verb candidates could have been chosen—serve God, fear God, obey God, trust God, worship God. Jesus intentionally chose love. And He didn't have to add the second commandment, and yet again He focused on love. He didn't say help, serve, tolerate, or forgive your neighbor; He said to love him as you love yourself. Love God, love others. So if we get love wrong here, we've missed the greatest commandment ever given. How important is it to understand love? Epic.

Jesus later raises the standard of love from loving your neighbor as yourself to loving others as He has loved us.

> A new commandment I give to you, that you love one another:
> just as I have loved you, you also are to love one another. By
> this all people will know that you are my disciples, if you have
> love for one another." (John 13:34–35)

This is a subtle but important shift. As humans we don't love
ourselves or others very well. We have lowered the love bar so that we
can easily step over it by our own preferences, opinions, and habits. Jesus
deliberately redefines love based on His own actions, not ours. His love
expressed through us should clearly separate the real Christ-followers
from posers.

Our understanding and practice of love repeatedly are put in the highest
place.[6] In 1 Corinthians 13, you can have and do many wonderful and
impressive things, but if you do not have love, you've really done nothing.[7]
In the "greatest" scales, love trumps even faith and hope.[8] In Colossians
and 2 Peter, love binds all the other virtues together.[9] In Ephesians, love is
to be sought, experienced, and practiced. In 1 John, love is the litmus test of
whether or not you are a Christ-follower.[10] Love is central to the Christian
life; neglect it at your own peril. In blunt language, do love or go to hell.

So, how important is your understanding of love? If love defines God,
if it is given by Jesus as the greatest commandment, if it's greater than any
other virtue, and if life without love is a death sentence, wouldn't you agree
that we better learn everything we can about this topic? Our knowledge
of love must also, of necessity, change the way we live. Believing in love,
understanding love, or even liking the concept of love is not the same as
doing love. As a Christ-follower, love should define who we are *and* what
we do.

Before we go forward, let me provide a short, simple working definition
for love: *Love is an intentional act for the good of someone else.*[11] This
definition is further clarified as a chosen way of being and acting as a
result of following Jesus Christ. It is more than merely a singular act, but
is a lifestyle. It is for the other person's good, even if there is no reciprocal
or positive response. Our starting point is that love is an action extended
to another person for his or her benefit.

A word of warning: Lest you think that "love one another" is one of the easier commands in the Bible, or certainly more politically-correct or less harsh, understand that the call to love is rigorously challenging.[12] It may sound quite simple and benign, but it is the costliest and most demanding of Christ's commands. Love is the root of the greatest commandment precisely because it is the most difficult and all-encompassing one. If we can get love right, all else will fall into place.[13]

The Dysfunctions of Unlove

The dysfunctions of human relationships are endless and virtually always the result of unlove. The ways we humans get love wrong are limitless and rampant, from love-poor families of origin to misdirected motives to outright acts of abuse (even in the name of love). We sometimes get love wrong by becoming a part of the problem instead of the solution, such as when benevolent acts become a condescending handout rather than a dignifying hand up. As humans, we have stuffed our inner lives with all sorts of baggage like hate, anger, prejudice, jealously, and pride. This inner dead weight is deeply rooted and limits our capacity to love.

Two of the most common ways that unlove rears its ugly head are through assault and withdrawal. Relationally, we opt for fight or flight. Assault includes the more obvious actions of abuse (all forms), power games, rage, ridicule, and even seduction. One's will is imposed upon the other person in an unloving way with no regard for the other's good. Withdrawal includes scorn, apathy, shunning, the silent treatment, and intentional disconnection. The other person is neglected and disregarded as undeserving of love; others are just not worth the effort. Most of our human problems today could be alleviated if simple love were to replace assault or withdrawal in relationships.

Where either assault or withdrawal is present, you can be assured that love is absent. In both cases, what is loving is withheld, and in its place, something destructive is substituted. And while the various forms of abuse may be more obviously evil to the casual observer, withdrawal and neglect over time also wreak significant relationship carnage. Unlove, in whatever form it takes, makes any relationship hazardous.

The core of the problem is that abusers and neglectors are love consumers. Their method is quite simple, if not lethal. They take what they want, when they want, and from whom they want. After they have had their fill of love's benefits at the expense of another person, they move on. Their consciences register no shame, guilt, or remorse. For them, unlove is natural and justified. Their actions are the opposite of do no harm. They strike and wound before "nicer" people are able even to defend themselves.

Imagine the scenario of Sam and Karen.[14] Without the counsel or blessing of his church leaders or friends, Sam married Karen within months of their meeting. Through Sam's influence, Karen started attending church again—something she had not done in years. Her previous marriage had taken her away from her childhood faith in Christ. Their first ten years together were a picture of marital bliss. Then over time, their relationship turned sour. Sam's language became hostile and his behavior unpredictable. Eventually, they sought counsel from their pastor and several professional counselors, but all to no avail. Sam hated telling others about their problems, while Karen loved the attention of venting his shortcomings to a listening ear. Karen attacked his character in public; he attacked hers in private. Assault and withdrawal were deeply embedded in their relationship pattern.

Sam became increasingly critical of his coworkers who offered help (attack). When confronted about his behavior, he would refuse to meet in person and wanted to drop the issue (withdrawal). Privately he would yell and intimidate Karen into submission and then offer her flowers and gifts for reconciliation (attack and withdrawal). Other times he would shut down all communication and sulk for days on end in his woodshop (withdrawal). Karen focused on her appearance; she joined a local gym, lost weight, and pursued the attention of successful men at her work place (withdrawal from Sam; attack on others). Karen eventually filed for a divorce because she did not feel loved by or safe around Sam. Sam and Karen's patterns of attack and withdrawal demonstrate unlove on several levels. Sadly, the pattern of this scenario is echoed in hundreds of relationships today, whether in the home or at the workplace.

Abuse and neglect have no justification in human relationships. Persons who are victimized should seek protection and help through caring people experienced in this area. By involving others, the victim acts for the abuser's good by introducing others who can help the victimizer. An unfortunate reality in life is that some people are so toxic with unlove and the relational damage they cause is so deep that their previous victims can only love them from a safe distance.

Narcissists are also included among the love consumers. Love requires selflessness, and narcissism is inherently self-centered. The narcissist not only wants to be loved but demands it. Like a black hole of condensed mass that sucks even light into its gravitational pull, so the narcissist drains love from others. The tragedy of the narcissist is that he or she has become incapable of love because the character has been so deformed into the image of self. Narcissists cannot love, even if they try.[15] They are deluded in their perceived adoration from others, and yet are actually the loneliest people in the world. The only hope for narcissists, as well as abusers and neglectors, is a complete reformation of their character by the grace of God.

The effective ploy that abusers, neglectors, and narcissists use is that they pretend to offer genuine love when, in fact, they are offering counterfeit love. Counterfeit love fakes others into believing that real love is actually being offered, but it is a guise to consume instead of give. Here the word *hypocrite* is most applicable because the appearance is that of giving love, but the reality is that of taking it. Their mask is love, but their heart and hands are unlove. Throughout Scripture, God's focus is always on the unity of the heart (character) and hands (actions), and that should also be our focus.

Love Short Happens

One of the more frustrating experiences in life is to come up short. It hardly matters what creates the occasion. It can be coming up short on cash at the end of the month. It can be coming up a quart low on paint and having to make another trip to the hardware store. It can be throwing horseshoes and getting nowhere near the stake. It can be that three-point shot that's an embarrassing air ball. If your pants are a little short, they're called high-waters. Coming up short means you don't have the coverage you need or want.

Short happens. Short happens with love as well.

When we try to base love on something that can't possibly give us the relationship coverage we need and want, we love short. For example, as a love hack I've learned that when I think I'm loving my wife well because my intentions are noble, I love short because my love lacks action. We love short when we are selfish or demand a reciprocal loving response out of others. We love short even when we "do love," if our motives are to be publicly recognized or to appear spiritually mature. Two areas in contemporary culture where we typically love short today are through feelings and tolerance.

More Than Feelings. By far, the most common responses I've received to the question, "What is love?" have included the idea of feelings. When the topic of love comes up, most people think of being in love instead of being a person who does the loving thing. Feelings so dominate us that one of our most frequent greetings is "How are you feeling?" This isn't a question of doing or even thinking, but of feeling. In our culture, feelings are paramount and take precedence over good thinking or ethical actions. We are so captivated by our emotions that if we don't *feel* love, then we *can't* or *shouldn't* love. We are never expected to violate our emotions by imposing action or thought on them. Disobedience to our emotions is the cardinal sin of the twenty-first century.

We will love short if we rely upon an emotion-driven model of love. Too often we're lulled into being in love with the feeling of love. When our goal is the feeling of love, we will soon be unable to do the things necessary for love. It's like exercising or eating a balanced diet. If you exercise and eat well, you will feel better in the long run. But if the short-term goal is to feel good, you won't push your body in the discipline of exercise or deny your body junk food. If I only exercise or eat well when I *feel* like it, I will not become physically fit, which in turn will not help me to feel better. Likewise, love has a discipline about it that pushes beyond our temporary feelings to do the things that make real love possible.

Feelings are unavoidable. Healthy emotions give a person a sense of well-being, even during difficult situations. Positive emotions *feel* great! And feelings, even bad ones, are preferable to a life without any feelings.[16] The primary reason, however, that love is not to be based on emotions is because feelings fluctuate; they are unreliable. Feelings may be good servants, but are bad masters. Emotions may provide a fantastic spark, but they are short on fuel. If you doubt me, did you know that the national divorce rate still hovers around fifty percent? Need further proof? How many people want the benefits of being married, but without the long-term sacrifice and commitment—i.e., are those who cohabitate?[17] Still not convinced? Why did you not marry the first person you were attracted to? The answer is that your feelings changed, and this is the main point here. Feelings alone will cause us to love short.

Nothing is cuter than puppies. They're playful, irresistible, and adorable. They evoke in us the emotions of wanting to take them home and nurture them. Sometimes a single glance from their sparkling, puppy eyes or a warm, friendly lick on the face triggers within us a strong emotional connection. They make us feel special. The only problem is that puppies grow up into dogs. After Fido digs up the flower bed for the third time in two weeks, chews up the cushions on the sofa, and then tracks in mud on your new carpet, new emotions emerge. The puppy love becomes doggy frustration.

Sadly, we treat many people in the same way. A new acquaintance seems like a great friend. The novel idea to get your family or friends serving at a soup kitchen is initially greeted with enthusiasm. The new person transferred in for a job opening looks to be a great fit for your company's sales team. Then time happens. With the passing of the weeks, the thrill fades. We no longer love our friend, love serving the poor, or love the new hire. Emotions shift, and then so do our relationships.

In stark contrast to emotion-based love, the Bible speaks of action-based love. In fact, God never tells us to *feel* love, but to *do* love. Our goal is no longer feeling happy, but simply loving God and others. We have erroneously convinced ourselves that our love is only legitimate and sincere if we feel it. From God's perspective, love is to be extended for the good of another person regardless of our feelings … even to those we do not like. We love when His love is forged in our character and chosen as an action. How, then, should we love people when we don't feel like it? C. S. Lewis's advice is sage.

> Act as if you did. Do not sit trying to manufacture feelings. Ask yourself, "If I were sure that I loved God, what would I

do?" When you have found the answer, go and do it … Do not waste time bothering whether you "love" your neighbor; act as if you did.[18]

Ultimately love isn't what you feel, but what you do.

More Than Tolerance. If one were to base his or her understanding of love on what is promoted through contemporary media, surely tolerance of one's neighbor would dominate. Christians are told to be more tolerant, and tolerance is held up as one of the higher expressions of love. In this view, love equals tolerance. In reality, tolerance is based on social apathy and selfish libertarianism. It says, "I really don't care what you think or do, so long as it doesn't inconvenience me." Tolerance can be legislated, monitored, and enforced; love will never stoop so low.[19] God doesn't merely tolerate you, He *loves* you.

Tolerance permits others to exist peacefully within your sphere of life, but does not require you to extend yourself to them in a loving way. In this sense, tolerance is the worst kind of love—near to others, but apathetic to their needs. Tolerance says, "I choose to leave you alone." Love says, "I choose to bless you." Tolerance closely guards relational boundaries; love reaches across them. Tolerance's motto, "Live and let live," is not the same as "I give myself sacrificially for your good." If one is motivated by the noble desire to not offend others (or the social fear of the same), she will not be able to love those who are different. Love does not seek to avoid the ire or annoyance of others, but seeks their good. Tolerance cautiously tiptoes on the perimeter, while love enters into the relationship with the offer of grace, patience, and kindness.

Perhaps the greatest test is this: Do tolerated people believe they are loved? They may feel patronized, ignored, or given a limited area in which to do their thing, but few feel loved.[20] Why is this? Because at its root, tolerance is apathetic, and apathy will never result in loving acts. Tolerance will respectfully do nothing to benefit the other person. Love, however, goes far beyond tolerance and the legal system. Love, by nature, chooses to actively do something for the other person's good. Genuine love will not expect or demand reciprocal "rights or entitlements." Love will extend itself sacrificially to even those that are different from, and even vehemently opposed to, you. Sadly, even many evangelical Christians who claim born-again status fall woefully short here. Not only is sacrificial love absent, but even tolerance is poorly offered.

Kara is a single mom who teaches English as a second language for international students at a local community college. The people in her classes come from every continent except Antarctica; every major world religion is represented. From outward appearances, her classes are models of peaceful, tolerant coexistence. In reality, her personal commitment to love people goes far beyond tolerance. She listens to her students, invites them to monthly theme parties, offers them free (donated) furniture, and helps them in whatever way she can. She has tea with Buddhists, attends cultural festivals at the Hindu temple, and visits the local mosque with the Muslims. She does not tolerate her students, even those with very different worldviews and from every different religious backgrounds—she loves them. She tangibly demonstrates love to them, and they know it.

Is there any hope for love hacks with a definition of love that's partial, anemic, and distorted? Is it conceivable to move beyond our emotions or sense of tolerance into what is really love? Is love even possible at all, or has this world been arranged in such a way that love will forever be longed for, but never achieved? We now turn our attention to the original source of love in the world.

CONFESSION OF A LOVE HACK

Ugly Feet

Beautiful Feet Ministries is compassionate outreach to the homeless of the Fort Worth metroplex. They provide a variety of services to at-risk and low-income people free of charge. Their church campus is off Vickery and Hattie in a declining industrialized area just south of downtown. Their name comes from the comforting words of Isaiah 52:7, "How beautiful upon the mountains are the feet of him who brings good news."

A friend of mine who volunteered there regularly invited me to preach on a Sunday morning. I was a young and unseasoned seminary student who had only preached a handful of times, and then mostly to empty chairs. Billy Graham or Billy Sunday I was not. I was more akin to Billy the Kid in the pulpit, a boy-faced minister killing innocent bystanders with impunity.

A date was set and I prepared myself for the momentous occasion. To complicate matters, in those days I worked ten-hour midnight shifts on Thursdays, Fridays, and Saturdays. By Sunday mornings, my brain and my body were toast ... burnt toast.

After I got off work at 7:30 a.m., I dressed up in my suit and drove my beautiful feet down to the church. I had polished my notes and practiced my sermon literally all night long. What could possibly go wrong? My rising career on the preaching circuit was about to launch!

And launch it did! A solid delivery of the gospel blew right through the crowd and fell flat on the concrete floor with a resounding thud. My eloquently garbled message had no traction with the rough lives of people on the streets. I sailed right over the heads of the poor and downcast; their hollow stares indicated that I had missed the mark. I fed spiritually starving people cotton candy ... all air and sugar, but no substance for malnourished souls.

Afterwards, one man who frequented the Sunday services had the courage to confront me. He addressed my pompous pretense and questioned my heart for the people. He wanted daily bread, not the fluff I was serving.

I wanted to look like a minister without being one. My unlove for the people in front of me was as big as my inflated ego inside of me. The more beautiful I tried to make myself look, the uglier my feet became. I was no longer bringing good, hopeful news about God's love and grace, but attempting to bring my goodness to the forefront.

Dear Jesus, forgive me for making my chief concern my own image instead of sharing your love with those who need it most. It's only as I follow Your crucified feet that mine become beautiful.

CHAPTER 3

In a World of Love

"The earth is full of the steadfast love of the Lord."
Psalm 33:5b

L'amour de Dieu est folie!
[The love of God is crazy!]
French Easter Liturgy

"God had so much love in him that he had to make us to get some love out."
Rachel, age 9

I have found that the world is generally made up of two kinds of people: people who like details and people who don't. Some people won't even take a new appliance out of the box until they've read the instructions and owner's manual; others pull it out and set it up without a second thought. Some of you are surprised that there is a thing called an owner's manual. This chapter is for those interested in the theological backstory of love's origin and what makes love possible. If this doesn't buzz your button, then skip to the next chapter. It's okay. Really. You have my permission. Your love will work just fine, even if you don't know why God made it so. For the rest of you, take a deep breath. We're going into some deeper water.

Imagine for a moment that you've just inherited a zillion dollars from a long lost uncle. The one stipulation in his will is that you must use the money to build yourself a dream home. You and you alone are responsible for selecting the location, the specific design, and the particular materials. Nothing can be delegated out to subcontractors except the actual labor of construction. Every detail of this massive project is yours, and the finished product would be a reflection of your character, creativity, and preferences. You may take as much time as you like in the design phase, but once construction begins, you will have only one year to complete it. For some of you, this would be a dream come true; others cringe at the demands of such detailed planning and management. But who wouldn't want the chance to give it a go?

The imaginary project that I've just outlined was accomplished by none other than God Himself on such a massive scale that it is inconceivable. He had an infinite amount of time to design. He had zero limits on materials to use. His location was quite large—astrophysicists have yet to determine the exact boundaries of the universe. To top it all off, He constructed it all in six days. And He didn't even need the financial backing of a rich uncle; He just spoke "stuff" into being as He desired and needed it. Pretty impressive!

Most of the time when we contemplate the world that God created, we think about things like snow-capped granite mountains, salty blue oceans, black Labradors, fluffy white clouds, buzzing bees, and colorful wildflowers. We think about the things we can see, touch, smell, taste, and hear. But rarely do we look beyond the seen to other unseen realities. The world that God created is indeed full of beauty, but it is also specifically designed for us to experience and express love.

The Trinity *Is* Love

Most of us have never seriously studied the Trinity—the understanding that the one God has revealed Himself in the three persons of God the Father, God the Son, and God the Holy Spirit. The Trinitarian understanding of God is distinctly Christian; no other world religion has a Trinity. Most pseudo-Christian cults distort this important perspective of how God has revealed Himself. Take away the Trinity, and we as Christians lose our unique understanding of God.

For our purposes here, I am not interested in some metaphysical or theological explanation of the Trinity, but I want to help us see how a proper grasp of the Trinity defines how we understand love. When the Bible says that "God is love," it isn't just talking about how God acts toward us, but it reveals something profound about God's nature and character as well. Love is who He is as well as what He does. His character and actions are perfectly united.

Contrary to the old erroneous view that the God revealed in the early stages of the Bible is full of wrath, the Old Testament repeatedly refers to the "steadfast loving-kindness of God."[1] In Psalm 136 alone, the phrase "His love endures forever" appears twenty-six times. God's love is steadfast and enduring. His love does not change. The New Testament simply affirms, continues, and clarifies this understanding of a loving God with the coming of Jesus Christ. Jesus is the tangible, physical proof of God's love for the world.

God is love. Love is a defining character trait in each person within the Godhead as well as the constant way that they relate to each other. For example, the Father loves the Son, and the Son loves the Father. Together they love the Holy Spirit. As all three persons lovingly interrelate to one another, all dimensions of love are expressed and experienced. Because love is such a foundational part of God's nature, He *is* love and *must* be loving.[2] He cannot not be love.[3] Love, like His holiness and goodness, just is.[4] Love is the divine way of relating to each other within the Godhead and to the rest of the world outside of the Godhead.[5]

Dallas Willard beautifully expresses the relational nature of God in Himself when he says,

> God is in himself a sweet society of love with a first, second, and third person to complete a social matrix where not only is there love and being loved, but also *shared* love for another, the third person. Community is formed not by mere love and requited love, which by itself is exclusive, but by *shared* love for another, which is inclusive. And within the Trinity there is, I believe, not even a thought of "First, Second, and Third." There is no subordination within the Trinity, not because of some profound metaphysical fact, but because the members of the Trinity *will not have it.*[6]

God intentionally acts for the good of others, even when the other is within Himself.[7] God's will is fixed in the position of freely choosing good for the other persons in the Godhead. And then collectively, the Godhead expresses that same love toward us. Because the Trinitarian God is a lover, He expresses love in everything He does and He makes all other loves possible.

On Earth as It Is in Heaven

In his attempt to reconcile the goodness of God with the suffering of the world, philosopher Gottfried Leibniz postulated that we live in "the best of all possible worlds." God in His infinite goodness created this world as the best of all possible worlds, and especially as it relates to how we the creatures can know God the Creator. This world in which we live—with all of its beauties and quirks, glories and sufferings—is the best of all possible worlds. It is also uniquely designed for heaven's love to be experienced here on earth.

Before God spoke the world into existence, He had all of eternity past to contemplate creation. He was under no deadlines; creation wasn't a rush job. He literally had an eternity to think through any kinks that may arise from design flaws. He had no budget constraints, no shortage of creativity, and no material limitations. God was absolutely free to bring the world into existence however He chose to do it. He was limited only by the proper constraints of His own nature and character.

Imagine for a moment what this would be like. He did not begin with a blank slate, but with no slate at all. He had only Himself. The "stuff" He might make could be totally spiritual and immaterial or something physical and visible. In the narrow spectrum of creation related to us humans, we could have been created as shimmering light shafts or only sound waves or preprogrammed with instincts or knowledge. He could have made us self-powered, or even robotic or as inert as a rock. We just as easily could have been created with ten legs, seven fingers, and purple skin. He didn't have to concern Himself with knockoff parts, profitability, or design flaws. He would only go into production when He could authoritatively say, "it was good."

"Good" in creation doesn't mean average, as in a few notches below better or best, but good as in thoroughly good—completely wholesome, without evil or flaws. In God's creation, there were no glitches in the program, no unforeseen bugs in the system. All risks were well-thought-out and accounted for in advance, even the eventual sin of mankind. This good world which God created *ex nihilo* (from nothing) was exactly what God wanted. This *is* my Father's world, and He made it in love.[8]

Part of God's perfect creative plan included us humans. Genesis 2:7 says that "the Lord God formed man of the dust from the ground and breathed into his nostrils the breath of life, and the man became a living creature." This combination of earth dust and God's breath formed a very complex being.[9] Several unmistakable features common to humanity are that we are physical beings capable of thought, communication, and relationships. What's more, when God made humans He intentionally made us in His image. "So God created man in his own image, in the image of God he created him; male and female he created them."[10] The image of God includes many possible aspects to it: intelligence, character, social dimensions, and the capacity to make decisions and rule, the ability to relate to God, and so on.

God's nature as love means that every part of His creative work flowed out of His good intentions for His creation. God made humans uniquely designed to receive and give love. As social and relational beings, we desire to communicate and connect with those outside of ourselves. As physical beings, the only way we can do that is through our human bodies. We are embodied souls that are hardwired for loving relationships.

It is as incarnational beings that we experience life … every single day without exception. We would do well to heed the advice of C. S. Lewis: "There is no good trying to be more spiritual than God. God never meant man to be a purely spiritual creature."[11] It is in my *body* that I live, experience, think, feel, and act. I cannot do otherwise. Even love—especially love—is an incarnational experience. This is simply God's arrangement of the world.

Before we leave our understanding of creation, take note of the "good" and "very good" of God's design. The world was created good. The creation of people was very good. God uniquely created man and woman in His image. God and people were able to communicate. God didn't want Adam to be alone so He created Eve—not merely as a sexual partner to complement him, but as a social partner ("it is not good that the man should be alone"[12]). Before the fall, Adam and Eve were completely free in receiving love from God and each other and able to give love to God and each other—without shame, without hindrance, without unlove. Eden was the place where love thrived on earth as it was in heaven.

Until they ate the forbidden fruit.

The fall of humanity into sin was also the fall into unlove. The two main movements of unlove quickly reared their heads: withdrawal and assault. The first movement was a withdrawal from God; Adam and Eve intentionally hid from God to cover their shame. When cornered, Adam attacked God and Eve: "the woman you gave me." When confronted, Eve attacked the snake, and as part of her punishment, her relationship with her husband would be contentious (as it would be with all the daughters of Eve). The curse of unlove settled in. In Genesis 4, Adam's now dysfunctional family continued the pattern of unlove. Cain attacked his brother Abel and killed him, and then Cain withdrew from God and became a social outcast. From the earliest of times, unlove became the history of the human race.

Love in the Fabric of Life

Being created in the image of the loving, Trinitarian God has significant implications for us today. As we become aware of them and embrace them, it will help us grow in how we love others.

Love and unlove are common to the human experience. Most psychologists agree that people have a real and deep need to be loved and to love. This need for love is innate at birth, and if love is not conveyed to a child in the earliest, formative stages, significant developmental issues arise. To love and be loved is a God-given drive and desire that the loving God of the universe put in the heart of mankind. The human hunger for love cannot be "satisfied by substitutes; it must be met."[13] Augustine said that "to be human is to love."[14] It's hardwired in to our relational DNA. The desire and need for love is universal.

Equally universal is the encompassing failure of love to be well received or well given. Even valiant attempts at love often end up in something less than ideal. The elusive nature of love is glaringly apparent in our culture due to the rates for divorce and abuse, the rise of social networking and attempts to connect socially, and the mere existence of blues and country-western music. More stories and songs can be shared about unlove than love. Love hacks still thrive. Adam and Eve's introduction of unlove has taken the course of human history down a painful path.

As frayed as it may be, the fabric of creation is love. This is why people from virtually every culture, race, and religion intuitively know that love is a better way of life than hate and apathy. This is why people pursue, even if quite imperfectly, the ideal of love. Muslims, Buddhists, Hindus, Africans, Asians, Indians, Europeans, and Latinos all know that love expressed through actions to others is good. In this regard, love is no secret virtue of Christians; it is God's gift to the whole world. Vestiges of God's love are still imprinted on the hearts of people everywhere.[15] Because of the way God designed creation, love is the one thing everyone wants and needs. Due to the introduction of sin into God's creation, love is the one thing that eludes us all. We thirst but remain parched. We hunger but are never sated.

Love must be expressed through our bodies. God's creation design is for us to be embodied. In fact, God's redemptive design for us is to be embodied as well—here on earth in our current bodies and in heaven in our resurrected bodies. The body is not evil per se, but a part of God's creation of being "very good." It is our misuse of the body that's the problem. We cannot exist without a form or body. Consequently, love cannot be received or expressed except through our bodies. The body is central to our basic existence.

When we sequester love to the "heart" of a person, we create an impossible scenario. Love must and will manifest itself through the body if indeed it is in the heart. The metaphysics aside, from a practical standpoint, the beloved never senses love until it is expressed tangibly, even if it is simply eye contact, facial expressions, or body language. Notice that eyes, faces, and bodies are obviously "bodily." Simply put, how do you know that someone loves you? They show it through the actions of their bodies.

A simple experiment can verify this: try to express love to your spouse, child, or friend without using your body. For this to be most effective and verifiable, the person cannot be aware that you are doing this experiment. First, you must not have a body. (Okay, so don't try that part of the experiment.) Second, you must seriously attempt to conjure up love in your heart—using your mind, will, and emotions. Third, now that you've got nice loving thoughts, motives, and feelings, transfer them to the other person, but without using a single part of your body—no speaking or writing, no facial expressions or body language. If possible, "telepath" your love to the person while you are not even in his or her presence. Fourth, ask the other person about his or her experience of your love. If that person is honest, he or she will not have even known you tried to love him or her. Love requires you to act through your body, and this is precisely how we receive love as well.[16]

I once offered the "Love Challenge" at our church. I offered one hundred dollars to the person who could demonstrate love without using his or her body to do it. Being Scottish, the thought of parting with a crisp Ben was terrifying. I had to be pretty convinced that this open wager would stand up to the test. Some tried; none succeeded. For us humans, a physical body is required for love to be made real.

God's adapts His revelation to us. Our creational design as embodied souls has direct consequences for how we know anything about God. God adapts His self-revelation to us. There are many ways we "incarnate" ones can understand God—voices, dreams, stone tablets, priests, prophets, and the indwelling Spirit. When God wants or needs to express love or truth to His people, He has several means at His disposal. We are made to communicate with God and the world around us.

In the days before Christ, people like Abraham experienced God in tangible ways—voices he could hear, smoking firepots, or strangers in human form. Jacob wrestled with God; how's that for a bodily experience of the divine! Moses knew God as a burning bush on the backside of the desert in Midian and then later spoke with God "face-to-face" on the top of Mount Sinai. In fact, the Jewish calendar began during this time so Moses could pinpoint the specific day that God spoke to Him. For the people of Israel, God appeared physically as a cloud by day and a pillar of fire by night. Repeatedly, the prophets could give the year, month, and day when they could say, "The word of the Lord came to me." In each circumstance, the messages and presence of God were delivered in such a way that these people knew God had intersected their lives. For God to even communicate with people, He condescended to our human level. In a very real sense, all revelation is adapted to us "incarnate ones."

When it came time for God to express the ultimate demonstration of His love, He didn't send another set of stone tablets, another message through a prophet, or another dream to interpret. No programs were established or a new temple complex constructed. God simply sent His one and only Son Jesus. John 3:16 says it succinctly: "For God so loved the world that He gave His one and only Son." When it came time for God to show humanity the fullest extent of His love, God sent an embodiment of Himself into the created world. If there could have been a better way, He would have done it. But because we're embodied, God sent an embodiment of Himself. All that we need to know about how to love God and others could now be seen, heard, touched, and expressed through the person of Jesus Christ.

God is love; it is His nature.[17] All of creation reflects God's love. We humans are specifically designed to receive and express love to and from God and other people. Love isn't foreign to the world. It's the foundation for all that is around us. Until we learn how to love God and others as we were originally designed, we will continue to experience various levels of unlove and imperfect love. Thankfully, God did not leave us without His most complete expression of love—Jesus Christ.

CONFESSION OF A LOVE HACK
Medal of Love

In the top of my closet, there's a box of miscellaneous personal items: my childhood dog's collar, an old baritone mouthpiece, photographs of my great-grandfather, a Coca-Cola can from the 1984 Los Angeles Olympics. Included in an old peanut can are my medals. These medals were awarded for things such as placing in swim meets, a baritone solo in the ninth grade, team triathlons, and karate tournaments. Most of my medals are pewter or bronze for third place or worse. One or two are silver. None is gold. I've succeeded in competitive mediocrity most of my life.

I've never received a medal for love. What's more, I've never come close to earning one. I've never even placed top ten. Even now as I "do love," I find dark and shadowy motives—pride, selfishness, desire for recognition, getting others indebted to me for my later benefit. My love still has strings attached; it is conditional and scheming.

Love hacks don't get love medals.

If there were a Medal of Love, what would it look like? In the military there's a pecking order for medals. The Purple Heart is fairly common and is awarded for being wounded or killed while in the line of duty. The Silver Star is the third-highest combat award for valor and heroism in the face of the enemy. The Distinguished Service Cross is the second-highest military award; it is not very common. The Cross is for those who instinctively risk their lives in an extraordinary way, usually while under fire and often to render aid to a fellow soldier. The Medal of Honor is the highest military decoration awarded and is extremely rare. It is bestowed by the president of the United States on behalf of Congress to the soldier who has distinguished himself by exceptional courage at clear and intentional risk to himself. It's for action that is obviously "beyond the call of duty." Often the Medal of Honor is awarded posthumously because the extraordinary action resulted in the sacrifice of the soldier's own life.

What kind of medal should be given to the person who performs an act of extraordinary heroism—knowingly and willingly and with much forethought and at grave personal risk—not for the sake of his friends, comrades, or allies, but for a known and hostile enemy? And he does it all because of love … for the other person's good? What if that very act of saving his enemies costs him his own life? The military has no medal for love of enemy because this borders on treason.

I propose that Jesus should be the sole recipient of the Medal of Love. He actually deserves it.

As it stands, I haven't earned any medals for love. If unlove were a sport, I might place. But fortunately for me, the heroic act of love that Jesus did on my behalf covers even my most hidden sins. This love hack's only hope is for the One who earned the Medal of Love to not only die for me, but to change me.

Dear Jesus, love me. And then love through me.

CHAPTER 4

Incarnational Love

In the beginning was the Word,
and the Word was with God, and the Word was God.
He was in the beginning with God.
All things were made through him,
and without him was not any thing made that was made …
And the Word became flesh and dwelt among us,
and we have seen his glory, glory as of the only Son from the Father,
full of grace and truth.
John 1:1–3, 14

"The life of Jesus is an act of love for others."
Scot McKnight

"Jesus is the most relatable expression of God we can know.
Reject him and you reject the one claiming the
clearest expression of God's personhood."
John Burke

*I*ncarnation isn't a word used in everyday life.[1] If we even think about it at all, we consider incarnation an abstract, theological word referring to the second person of the Trinity—Jesus—taking on His humanity during His time on earth. Perhaps we give it a gentle nod at Christmas with all the emphasis upon the sweet baby Jesus. Rarely do we think as concretely about it as we should. Without the incarnation, we have no Jesus. Without the incarnation, we have no us. Both Jesus and we are incarnated … made to have a human body and put here on earth.

The singular person in the history of the world to tangibly and perfectly demonstrate a life of love is Jesus. Apart from whatever bad press His followers may give Him, He still remains the supreme example of love in His teachings, actions, life, and death.

Nobody has, or ever will, out-love Jesus. Nobody. If we are to love, we would do well to look deeply into how Jesus loved.

The Incarnation of Jesus

John's gospel begins with powerful words about the Word.

> In the beginning was the Word, and the Word was with God, and the Word was God. He was in the beginning with God. All things were made through him, and without him was not any thing made that was made. (John 1:1–3)

Words, commonly understood, are the way that thoughts are expressed (whether written or spoken). Who or what is this Word? How do we know that John was referring to Jesus instead of God's own voice or the way God spoke through prophets of old? Here the Word—who was God and an active part of creation—does something that no other word had ever done. The Word became human; it took on a human body. The Word walked and lived on earth.

> And the Word became flesh and dwelt among us, and we have seen his glory, glory as of the only Son from the Father, full of grace and truth. (John 1:14)

This Word was the glorious Son of God, brimming full of grace and truth. John testifies that he and others actually saw this "human Word" with their own eyes. This is the great mystery of Christmas: God manifested physically in Jesus.[2]

The apostles had the best seats in the house to observe firsthand the life of Jesus. As His students and closest followers, they spent enormous amounts of time together. In reference to Jesus, the apostle John says:

That which was from the beginning, which we have heard, which we have seen with our eyes, which we looked upon and have touched with our hands, concerning the word of life—the life was made manifest, and we have seen it, and testify to it and proclaim to you the eternal life, which was with the Father and was made manifest to us—that which we have seen and heard we proclaim also to you, so that you too may have fellowship with us; and indeed our fellowship is with the Father and with his Son Jesus Christ. (1 John 1:1–3)

In this brief intro, John emphasizes over and over that Jesus appeared *physically*. He could be seen, touched, and heard. Jesus was the most accessible God had ever become. Jesus wasn't simply another guy pointing others to God; *He was God in the flesh*. Divine revelation could be experienced tactilely. In Christ, God's love became "touchable." He didn't merely teach love theory, but He lived it out in the ordinary conditions of everyday human life.[3]

God did not "tweet" His love to us. He did not send a book or DVD. He didn't ask us to download an iTunes or give us blueprints for a new temple. God sent His love in the form of a living, breathing person. A "spiritual presence" of the Unmoved Mover simply would not do. A Suffering Lover in a human body was the only way we could know God was really there—physically present—for us.

Yet even His disciples struggled with such a tangible expression of God. At the last meal Jesus shared with His closest followers, Philip still doesn't quite "get" the incarnation.

Philip said to him, "Lord, show us the Father, and it is enough for us." Jesus said to him, "Have I been with you so long, and you still do not know me, Philip? *Whoever has seen me has seen the Father.* How can you say, 'Show us the Father'? Do you not believe that I am in the Father and the Father is in me? The words that I say to you I do not speak on my own authority, but the Father who dwells in me does his works. Believe me

that I am in the Father and the Father is in me, or else believe
on account of the works themselves. (John 14:8–11; emphasis
added)

What was it that Jesus visually expressed about God? Was it harsh
condemnation and judgment? Was it higher standards for low morals?
The Word that was made flesh was specifically the love of God. "God so
loved the world that He gave His one and only Son."⁴ How does God tell the
world of His love? Through actions ... through giving His Son.

Jesus is love at ground zero. He is the epicenter of love at its most
tangible, clearest, and strongest expression in history.

He Walked Among Us

One of the greatest things that the incarnation of Jesus teaches us is
that the love God intends is surprisingly adapted to human life. It requires
no out-of-body experience, just a willing person in a body. Jesus' every day
actions were a constant display of God's love. Those actions seamlessly fit
into the world in which He lived.

I have traveled enough internationally to know that simply being in
a foreign country physically isn't enough to connect with the locals. A
functional use of the language and a working knowledge of local customs
are indispensable. To really "be there," you have to become one of them.
When you're not well versed in a culture, it's glaringly obvious that you're
the outsider.

During my first trip to France, I was virtually clueless about the nuances
of the French language and even more so about their unspoken customs.
My mother tongue and native culture is Texan with Okie overtones. While
on crowded Parisian sidewalks and in the Metro (subway), I replied *"Merci"*
when bumped and jostled. I thought I was apologizing for accidently
touching a stranger. Was I ever wrong! *Merci* means "thank you," not "I
beg your pardon." You can only imagine the odd looks I was getting from
people! It wasn't until three days into the trip that my wife overheard my
faux pas and gave me a quick lesson in French 101. Though present in
France, I was never really a part of French life.

When Jesus came to earth, He fully incarnated. He didn't butcher the language and violate social norms (although He clearly critiqued religious errors). He completely embraced the life, customs, language, and habits of a first-century Jew. The question that people raised after meeting Jesus was not "How can this God be so human?" rather "How can this man be God's Son?" His divinity was the shocker, not His humanity. He was so "like us" that it wasn't until after His resurrection that people stumbled over His humanity.

Jesus operated out of a love relationship with His heavenly Father. Throughout His public ministry, Jesus tangibly knew of God's love. At His baptism, the voice from heaven boomed with "This is my beloved Son." Early on, twice Jesus affirmed, "The Father loves the Son." During His transfiguration, Jesus again heard the words, "This is my beloved Son." Weeks before His death, He still affirmed, "The Father loves me." Even during His last evening before His death, Jesus said, "As the Father has loved me ...."[5] Like a drenched sponge that drips out water when moved, so Jesus was saturated with the Father's love throughout His life. Jesus loved because He Himself was loved.

When Jesus loved others, what did He actually do? What does love look like? It's pretty hands-on and personal.

In third-world conditions in a pre-modern environment, Jesus' love was quite germy. He did not flinch in expressing love—skin-on-skin—with all kinds of people. Find your favorite sterile plastic bubble and meditate on who He actually touched: people with lice, open sores, leprosy, and sexually transmitted diseases. He physically rubbed shoulders with toothless widows, smelly fishermen, rustic shepherds, drooling babies with dirty (non-disposable) diapers, unwashed demoniacs, and soiled, bed-ridden paralytics. He put His fingers literally in the ears of the deaf, on the eyes of the blind, and on the soles of disciples' feet. He did it all without rubber gloves and hand sanitizer. Love thrives even in unsanitary conditions.

His presence was so real that not only did He touch people physically, but they touched Him. Crowds would press against Him in hopes of a healing miracle or of touching One who seemed so full of life and love. Many times when Jesus was expressing God's love and forgiveness, others would reach out for Him. The "sinful woman" expressed her gratitude for forgiveness by washing Jesus' feet with her tears and drying them with her hair. An older woman with an incurable menstrual condition grabbed the tassel of His tallit. A former demoniac latched on to His feet in appreciation for his newfound deliverance and freedom. Mary, the sister of Martha and Lazarus, "wasted" a vial of expensive perfume on Jesus in an extravagant act of love for Him. Jesus' body was available as a source of love as well as a place to give love back to God.

Beyond physically being present to people, Jesus expressed love in a variety of ways. He spoke life-giving words to crowds. He had private conversations with closet inquirers such as the Pharisee Nicodemus. He taught His disciples privately in strategic retreats. In love He spoke and listened. He fed hungry people—four thousand men (not including the women and children) on one occasion and over five thousand in another. He ate with notorious sinners, tax-collectors, and prostitutes. He healed the sick, cast out evil spirits, cleansed lepers, straightened backs, and strengthened paralytics.

When Jesus walked on earth, He walked slowly and deliberately. He was the physical incarnation of God's love, and that love was active.[6] Whenever Jesus had compassion, it always erupted into actions … every single time. He put the *do* in do love.

When it comes to love, my mind struggles to grasp the fact that Jesus never sinned. His love was always perfect every single day. As a love hack, I rarely make it past noon before I've blown my love assignments for the day. Whether seething because of some jerk driver who cut me off in traffic or some brainless oaf who packed twenty-seven items in the express lane of the grocery, love in everyday life is tough. Selfishness comes very naturally to me; my wife and kids can testify that my words, decisions, and general demeanor have too often been about me. Jesus never acted selfishly or even thought in selfish terms. He was always patient and kind, never allowing irritation and frustration to boil over into sin. He lived in a fallen world among sinful people who had a limited capacity for love. Yet He never acted sinfully or contributed to the sin of the world.

Most of us have toyed with the self-revealing, theoretical question, "If you could have dinner with three people from any point in history, who would you pick and why?" If you're a "good" Christian, you feel obligated to say that one of your guests would be Jesus. I think that an experience with Jesus face-to-face would be tremendously insightful. I imagine the love that would ooze out of Him would be palatable. We all think how wonderful it would be just to bask in His goodness and love. Like the adoring, fawning crowds at the triumphal entry, we'd wave our palm branches, smile toothy grins, and throw in a few "Hallelujahs."

But only for a moment. Until we really realize how loving He is and we are not. Until we fail to get our way and melt down with a defiant tantrum. Until we realize the only way to stop the awareness of our unlove is to either change ourselves or kill Him. Like Jesus' contemporaries, death of another is preferable to death of self.

Don't think for a minute that it wouldn't happen again if you had only been there. Compared to Jesus, we're all love hacks. Left to ourselves, we'll all try to hack Him down to our size, even if it means murder. In the presence of pure love, unlove's first impulses are assault and withdrawal … to betray and then flee … to deny and then hide … to kill and then bury. We are all born with the automatic default of unlove; it's hardwired into our spiritual genetics.

"No Greater Love"

Not only was Jesus' life a stunning visual display of God's love through countless acts of compassion to specific hurting and needy people, but also His death was the supreme tangible expression of God's love for all people.[7] Romans 5:8 is crystal clear: Jesus died to express God's love. "God demonstrated his love for us in this, while we were still sinners, Christ died for us." The sacrifice of God and His Son was not "in theory" or an abstract theological principle, but was a divine event in time and space. It was real suffering with real blood … a real death with real nails on a cross of real wood. Nowhere does the incarnation of Christ get more physically grisly than with His death.

God's motivation for expressing love is quite simply that He could do no other. God *is* love, therefore "God so loved the world that He gave His one and only Son." God didn't have reasons that existed outside of Himself, as if God owed it to us because we were deserving of love or simply because we were needy. Actually, the Bible is quite silent on the "why" behind God's love other than the fact that love is His nature and choice.

Love always comes as a gift. It needs no reason because it *is* its own reason. God's love is scandalous because it is free and undeserved.

Although Jesus' act of love on the cross benefitted us, His motivation was His love for His heavenly Father. Both in life and in death, Jesus showed His love to the Father through simple, uncomplicated obedience.[8] No better place do we see Jesus' submission to His Father in simple obedience than in His Gethsemane prayer: "Abba, Father, all things are possible for you. Remove this cup from me. Yet not what I will, but what you will."[9] Love for God says, "My life is not about me, but about You. I love you so much that I want Your will done more than mine." What makes this prayer so powerful are not the words alone, but the reality that Jesus followed it up with the sacrifice of His own life.

Simple obedience should not be confused with or understood as being easy. Simple and uncomplicated means that Jesus viewed His life through a streamlined approach:

- I know that God loves Me.
- God tells Me what to do because He loves Me.
- I do what He says because I love Him.

For Jesus, love was distilled down to obedience to the Father's will.[10] Jesus' love for God was always preeminent—it was before every other love. Yet His love for God was expressed in the greatest love act of a Man for men. Jesus died because He loved God, but His love for man was no less. He died because He loved us, too.

> Greater love has no one than this, that someone lay down his life for his friends. (John 15:13)

Jesus appeared in a body for the purpose of taking away our sins. He laid down His life for all of us.[11]

When traveling abroad, I enjoy a side trip to the local markets. In many Asian markets as well as in many tourist locations in Europe, vendors sell knockoff "name-brand" fashion apparel, accessories, and electronics. Some of them are dead giveaways: Gucchi (Gucci), Rolax (Rolex), or Norfh Face (North Face). Sometimes the only telltale sign is the price. A Rolex watch for $30, really? A Louis Vuitton purse for $18? Being a Scottish tightwad, such deals are hard for me to pass up. As a recovering love hack, I'm learning that love calls for the highest sacrifice, not the lowest bid. Nothing says "You're not worth it" like a shoddily sewn "Pollo" shirt. Nothing says unlove quite like a Rolax watch that loses four minutes a day. When God the Father offered His one and only Son, it was no knockoff gift. When the Son offered His life to accomplish the Father's will, it wasn't at bargain prices. Both actions were God's expression of His costly and precious love for us.

Jesus' death on the cross for us is the gold standard for all other loves; it defines love as the ultimate selfless sacrifice.

> By this we know love, that he laid down his life for us, and we ought to lay down our lives for the brothers. (1 John 3:16)

> In this the love of God was made manifest among us, that God sent his only Son into the world, so that we might live through him. In this is love, not that we have loved God but that he loved us and sent his Son to be the propitiation for our sins. (1 John 4:9–10)

In an ultimate showdown with the world's unlove, Jesus Christ paid the highest price for making sure that God's love was clearly and tangibly expressed through His death. Unlove could only be overcome by Love.

"I Love You Forever"

I must confess that I've always been a little leery of the word "love." In junior high when I intercepted love notes that were passed across the aisle in algebra class, I was always baffled by how frequently the word "love" was scribbled on scraps of paper along with generous drawings of hearts. When "I'll love you forever!" was written by a giddy thirteen year old girl,

I was thinking, "Yeah, right! And you've already committed your 'forever love' to four different guys since lunch." Superficial phrases of immature, infatuated love still give me a visceral reaction akin to nausea.

Forever love—that's what we're all after, isn't it? Love is a big enough word, but with forever as a qualifier, I must gracefully bow out. Even when this phrase is used in a wedding ceremony, it's awkwardly out of place. Physical death severs the bond of marriage. The vows are "till death do us part," not "forever and ever, Amen." The feelings of love may linger long after the death of our beloved ones, but our opportunity to show love vanishes when their physical bodies cease to be alive.

Fortunately for us, God's love not only trumps shallow infatuation, but is also greater than even married love. The life and death of Jesus for us was certainly a bright spot in time when God demonstrated His love for us. But Jesus died. Didn't that put an end to His love?

Easter is the emphatic *yes* of God to life and *no* to unlove.

One of the oft overlooked truths about Jesus' resurrection is that it establishes a *forever* love relationship with God. Unlike teenage sappy love that says, "I love you forever," but has no possible way to back it up, when God says, "I love you forever," He bases it again upon a tangible act in history—the resurrection of Jesus Christ from the dead. God's love for us will not fade with time, but remains perpetual, real, and alive as in the first century when Jesus lived and loved here on earth.

The cross of Jesus says, *I love you.* His resurrection adds, *forever.* Together they give us the basis to affirm that nothing can "separate us from the love of God in Christ Jesus our Lord" because "God's love has been poured into our hearts through the Holy Spirit who has been given to us."[12] Poured. To the brim. Overflowing. Lavishly wasted on us.[13]

Receive this forever love. Rest in it. For in God's love you will find the source for all other loves. "We love because he first loved us."[14]

CONFESSION OF A LOVE HACK
Black Holes

Do you want to know a dirty little secret that pastors have? In the big scheme of things, it may be worse than hidden liquor in the study or a monthly foray into internet porn. The hush-hush? We don't love all people. We certainly don't like all people.

In backrooms at pastors' conferences, away from recording devices and non-clerical ears, there's honest confession that some people in the church drive us crazy. They go by different names: ELR (extra love required), love leeches, time eaters, the "crazy" one, Mr. Hot Air or Mrs. Needy, or some cases simply deacon.

These folks are the black holes of ministry. They suck every shred of love into their gravitational pull. They ask for three minutes and take seventy-four. They tell stories of doom, gloom, and woe with such skill that empathy for their cause is elicited and we, the listening ear of love, are manipulated into cheap compliments and obliged sympathy.

We have what they want—attention, praise, hope, and most importantly, unconditional love. We're pastors. As shepherds of God's flock, we have to love them, right? Our job is to listen attentively, pat their hand, and say, "Everything's going to be fine."

The courageous person who attempts to create relational boundaries is slandered as being an overly busy cog in the heartless machine of the modern church. The brave soul that tries to confront with truth in love is first doubted, then demonized, and finally run out of town.

So what are pastoral love hacks to do? Spend their days dodging sheep? Smile, nod empathically, and say sweet nothings? Or pray like crazy that our hearts would be changed?

Lord, instead of saving me from black holes of ministry, save me from a shrinking heart that avoids opportunities to love others in the way you do.

CHAPTER 5

Love Tank

"God's love has been poured into our hearts through
the Holy Spirit who has been given to us."
Romans 5:5b

Quia amasti me, fecisti me amabilem.
[In loving me, you made me lovable.]
St. Augustine

"I can live without money, but I cannot live without love."
Judy Garland

*B*ig Bend National Park is a massive wasteland in the Chihuahua
Desert along the Texas-Mexico border. At over 800,000 acres, it's
larger than Rhode Island. It's one of the most remote and least visited
national parks in the United States. Back in the '90s, I got this brilliant
idea to solo hike from the Chisos Mountain Basin to the Rio Grande
River—about a thirty-five mile trip with few trails and no paved roads.
I was longing for some solitude with God and to decompress from my
graduate studies. My friend, Jonathan, an amateur photographer, would
provide the drop-off and pick-up.

The area that I planned to trek was so remote that the park rangers
not only require hikers to register at the park headquarters, but they also
make note of the color of their clothes and tent. They even took a chalk
imprint of the sole of my boot.[1] They calmly said, "Just in case ... standard
procedure."

At noon Jonathan dropped me off at the trailhead and promised to meet me in Castolon in two days. He asked if there were any final words to pass on to my wife and sons, "just in case." The first seven miles were all uphill to the rim of the basin. From there, I enjoyed a panoramic view of the surrounding desert before descending an overgrown trail to the dry creek beds below that eventually found their ways to the Rio Grande. Dry was the operative word. Dry as in no water to filter and refill the canteen.

Three things worked against me early on: a hot midday start, an uphill climb, and an overloaded pack. As the evening sun was moving westward, I realized that I had sucked down more than my anticipated ration of water. I did some quick math and realized that at the current pace of walking and drinking, I would not have enough water to make the trip.

My prayer life increased exponentially with a gnawing panic in the back of my mind. Solo hikes have a small margin for error—potential hazards are already significant. Being dehydrated makes clear decision making murky. Water became an obsession. Visions of slowly desiccating in the Texas sun blurred my vision. Backup plans were schemed—"just in case ... standard procedure."

There was one small point on the topographical map that indicated a deserted building not far from a park road. While still a mile away, I could hear faint voices floating over the desert rocks. Out of desperation, I changed routes with the hope that perhaps I could mooch some water from these "car tourists." By the time I arrived, the Blue Creek Ranch house was a ghost town: an arid, lonely stone and adobe hut. My hopes for water evaporated.

My prayers were now turning from repetitive pleas for help to snarky remarks under my breath. My sarcastic comments went something like, "Thanks, God, for taking care of me out here in the middle of nowhere. Now that I have no water, I really appreciate your care and concern." About mid-sentence of the fourth complaint, my foot kicked a two-liter bottle of water—just sitting there waiting for me. Some gracious, unnamed person from Whitney, Texas had left a bottle of filtered water. This was literally and tangibly God's gift of love to me.

Here's what I know: God's love is like cool, clean water in the desert. You don't just want it, you need it. Survival depends on it. God's love isn't optional for the believer.[2] Unlove equals dysfunction and death.

Drink Deeply

Many people go through life without an awareness of God's love, much less with a life-changing experience of it. They sense the deep longing within to be loved and to share love, but the longing is never fully satisfied. Their life stories are filled with painful experiences of friendship betrayals, one-night stands, child abuse, and a sequence of failed relationships. False starts, not finish lines, describe their love life.

Jesus met such a love-thirsty woman by a well in Samaria.[3] Jesus needed water; she needed love. As the conversation unfolded, Jesus pointed out that her human love experiences had been serially insatiable—she had five botched marriages and was currently living with a sixth man who likely didn't respect her or care enough to marry her. She was used goods. She was not thriving, but barely surviving. Listen carefully to what Jesus offered:

> Jesus said to her, "Everyone who drinks of this water will be thirsty again, but whoever drinks of the water that I will give him will never be thirsty again. The water that I will give him will become in him a spring of water welling up to eternal life." (John 4:13–14)

Later Jesus repeats this theme of life-giving water in John 7 when He says:

> "If anyone thirsts, let him come to me and drink. Whoever believes in me, as the Scripture has said, 'Out of his heart will flow rivers of living water.'" Now this he said about the Spirit, whom those who believed in him were to receive, for as yet the Spirit had not been given, because Jesus was not yet glorified. (John 7:37b–39)

The Spirit that Jesus offers is life-giving. Like graciously given water to a thirsty man, the invitation to come and drink deeply of His love is offered.

Brennan Manning says that "Christians find it easier to believe that God exists than that God loves them."[4] I believe him. I even think that many would more easily believe that the moon really is made of cheese than to embrace the love of God. The one thing we need most is the one thing we refuse. We reject the invitation to drink in His love while at the same time we slowly die of spiritual dehydration. What's worse, we blame our shriveled souls on God.

Does this sound like a God who is stingy with His love: "God's love has been poured into our hearts through the Holy Spirit who has been given to us"?[5] What's the common denominator in "spring of water welling up," "flowing rivers," and "poured out?" Love is offered in abundance, in excess. God doesn't dole out a thimbleful of water with resentment. He fills up the ocean and invites us in for a refreshing swim!

Have you ever experienced the pounding surf of the ocean that knocks you off your feet or powerful riptides that carry you out to deeper water regardless of how much you strain against the currents? Because of our fear of drowning in God's love, we cautiously set up our picnic on the shore and never get more than our toes wet. We'd rather be underwhelmed by safe sand than overwhelmed by the risky water of love.

But God calls us into the deep … not to kill us, but to give us life. His love equals our life.

Exactly how do we make the eighteen-inch transition from knowledge of God's love that's in our heads to the experience of God's love in our hearts? We know that God loves people, even if we don't think He really loves us personally. Loving people is a part of His job description as God, right? Isn't it clear that the Bible says that "God so loved the world?"

Four things are required on our part to position ourselves under the love spout of God.[6] *First, we must acknowledge our need.* The feeling of thirst is a gift that our bodies provide to tell us that we need water. The experience of thirst may not be pleasant, but it's an important signal that we shouldn't ignore. If we don't heed the sign, we'll never get our real need met. While hiking, I had to acknowledge that I was low on water and needed more. Our needs are intended by God to direct us back to Him. "Without needs we cannot experience love—we cannot know when we are being loved …. Need gives us the capacity to feel loved."[7] The sooner we see our need for love as a gift from God, the sooner will we seek to have that need met through Him. Augustine said, "You have created us for Yourself, and our heart is not quiet until it rests in You."[8]

Second, we must have the humility to turn to God to meet our love needs. Even after we admit that we're love thirsty, we must have the humility to receive the love offered to us from God. Typically the greater our thirst, the more open we are to outside help.[9] I was willing to change my hiking route, approach total strangers, and beg for water when I was near the Blue Creek Ranch. When we recognize our desperate need for love and see love offered to us in Christ, that is not the time to arrogantly critique it. The smart thing to do is drink the life-giving water, not pass on it with an air of false humility. Desperate people aren't in a position to be smug sommeliers, but are in a perfect place to greedily drink life-giving love until their thirst is quenched.

Third, we must trust that what is offered is really given. This is where love and faith intersect. I must trust that when God says I am loved in Christ Jesus that He is telling the truth … that His love is a reality. I must trust in Him so much that I *act* loved. There was a moment of truth when I picked up the two-liter gift of water that I had to decide—drink from a strange source or be thirsty? I had to trust in Mr. Unknown from Whitney, Texas that the water was not tainted. As a love hack, trust doesn't come easily for me. I don't mind giving so much, but being in the needy place of trusting is relationally awkward for me. The following words from Bill Thrall and Bruce McNicol stopped me cold in my tracks one day.

> *The degree to which I trust you is the degree to which I am able to receive your love, no matter how much actual love you may try to give me.* People unable to trust will never experience love—not ever.[10]

It was the "not ever" that slammed me. For me to experience God's love means I must trust Him—really trust Him. Trust Him so much that I act like I am loved. If He says that He loves me with a lavish, crazy love, then who am I to argue with the God of the universe? I should trust His character, words, and actions. And the evidence of me trusting in Him is actually taking that first drink of love.[11]

Fourth, we must drink deeply. When we are love-thirsty, what we need is not a mouthful of water, but gallons and gallons. Forget high-browed, civilized sipping; slurp and gulp like the dying person you are. When I finally committed to drinking the water found on my hike, I drank all two liters. I didn't leave a drop behind. Take in all of the love that God offers to you in Jesus Christ. Read and re-read the passages that speak of God's love. Like the returning prodigal, let the Father throw a party in celebration of your homecoming. God comes to you with His grace face. It's not about you being perfect, but about learning to receive His perfect love.[12]

When you have experienced serious thirst and have it slaked with plenty of cool water, you don't merely feel better, you *are* better. A core need of your body is satisfied. Feeling normal is the byproduct of being hydrated. The same is true for experiencing God's love. What your soul needs is God's love. When you experience it, you feel better because you *are* better.[13] When the Bible says that "God's love has been poured into our hearts through the Holy Spirit," think of an unending flow of life-giving water that makes you spiritually alive and healthy.

The Love Tank

As a kid growing up in West Texas, when the gas gauge bordered on empty my dad would pull his 1964 Chevy station wagon into his favorite Fina station to "fill 'er up with the cheap stuff." Even people who don't know a head gasket from a fuel injector are sharp enough to know that without gas a car won't start much less take you anywhere. No fuel means no go—even if you crank the key, drain the battery, and cuss the motor. In fact, your car blissfully disregards all of your antics until you meet the basic conditions necessary for starting it. If you want your love motor to "run," it has to be provided with the necessary conditions for this to happen. God's love is that fuel.

God's love is not "the cheap stuff." He doesn't offer us the lowest-grade octane to run our lives at the minimum horsepower possible. His love is premium grade—like expensive rocket fuel compared to the gas you put in your vehicle at the convenience store. Though the love of Christ is offered freely, it does not come cheaply. We are able to love because the love we receive is first-rate. His love is so wide, long, high, and deep that it's beyond our comprehension.[14] This love is what we were designed to use when we love God and others.

Imagine for a moment that you have a large, deep vat. It has an open top and several small holes along its sides. This is your love tank. If your tank is full, love will drain out the side holes to bless other people. If your tank is empty, only unlove will come out. In the simplest of terms: you give what you have. You cannot give away what you don't have.

If your love tank is brimming full with the love of God because you've discovered how to place yourself under His spigot to daily top off the tanks, you have plenty of love to share with people around you.[15] If your love tank is dry or has only inches of love, you will scoff at and resent the idea of giving yourself away on someone else's behalf. If you have no love inside of you, you have no love to give away outside of you.

Understand that in this illustration, love doesn't just exist "out there"—as if it were an entity apart from God or some impersonal cosmic vibe in the universe. God is the sole reason and source for love; He *is* love. Love isn't a stand-alone virtue that is detached and independent from God. Love is an action initiated by God and people. Therefore, God fills our love tanks because He is love and demonstrates His love to us. We, in turn, love God back and love other people because of His presence in our lives. Incarnationally speaking, the love of the invisible God is given *to* us and *through* us visible people. We are to be the hands, feet, and voice of Jesus here on planet Earth—this is why we are called the body of Christ.

Before we focus on how to "do love," we must first make sure that we are squarely under the spigot of God's love. Exactly how do we place ourselves in a position to daily experience a fresh refilling of love from God? It's not rocket science or brain surgery. How often do you drink liquids a day? Just as you keep yourself physically hydrated every day through sporadic drinks throughout the day, in the same way keep yourself spiritually hydrated by drinking regularly from the love God offers you in Christ.

Let me give you a hint: a once-a-week trip to church will keep you about as healthy as a once-a-week drink of water. Regardless of how much love from God you drink in a single sitting, you can't possibly drink enough to maintain any sense of spiritual health to cover the next six days. There is something powerful and wonderful that happens when believers gather for worship, encouragement, and to hear a word from God. However, when it comes to personally experiencing the love of Christ, daily—even moment-by-moment—downloads of love from God will keep your love tank filled.[16]

By looking at the life of Christ and how He maintained a full love tank, we see that He often retreated away from others to have time alone with God. Even Jesus didn't try to give away what He did not have. In His private prayers, Jesus made sure that He was hearing clearly and obeying fully His heavenly Father.[17] His was a surrendered life. For us with sin, we could add to our prayers the regular confession of sin and recalibrating of our souls to the life of Jesus Christ. This should happen daily through intentional time, but it also should be happening regularly through the normal flow of our day. We pause, check in with our heavenly Father, reaffirm His love for us, and then obediently love others. As we regularly receive love, we are able to regularly give it away.

Open Wide

When most of us hear the words, "Open wide," we have nightmarish flashbacks of being strapped in the dentist's chair with a masked stranger putting latex-tasting fingers and sharp metal objects in our mouths. Like Pavlov's dogs, when we hear "open wide," we instinctively tense up and squeeze the nearest armrest with a Vulcan death grip. This is not the picture of peace and replenishment God intends when He says, "Open your mouth wide, and I will fill it" (Psalm 81:10b). God's not a cruel sadist who delights in inflicting pain on us. He loves us more than any one else, and His goal is to provide us with all the love we need. When our spiritual mouths are open, God generously fills it with good things. He refills our love tanks with Himself; our job is to make sure that our love tank lids are wide open in God's direction.

If you've ever seen a nest of hatchling robins in the spring, you know that those baby birds are ravenous and demanding. Whenever Mr. or Mrs.

Robin touches the nest, the hatchlings throw back their heads and open their mouths as wide as possible. The parents relentlessly stuff partially-chewed insects and worms down their gullets (yuck!). The chicks' hunger is shameless and insatiable. This is precisely the picture we need of God and us. He is providing the spiritual nourishment of His love that we desperately need to live and grow. We are to recklessly open our mouths as wide as possible for the maximum love download.

By contrast, have you ever tried to feed a picky eater, such as a stubborn toddler who despises vegetables? You can slip him into a straightjacket, strap him into a highchair, and even make airplane noises for the incoming green beans, but if he's determined to be tight-lipped, no amount of coaxing will pry apart his clenched jaws. Just because there's a pantry full of nutritious food and a willing parent to offer it doesn't mean that the child benefits from what's available. This, too, is an instructive image of our relationship with God. He freely offers love and spiritual nourishment for our good, but if we clamp our spiritual mouths tighter than a steel trap, *whatever* God offers us will be of no use to our souls. God doesn't force-feed us, but offers a daily banquet of love. We—not God—are responsible for opening our mouths wide. His job is to abundantly fill the open mouths.

The first two stages of the love flywheel are crucial here. Exactly how do we see and experience the love of Christ so that we can give away what we've received? How does one spiritually "open wide?" Here are a few suggestions to get you started.

Bible: Since seeing the love of God in Jesus is crucial, the Bible obviously is our primary source. Daily read, study, memorize, and/or meditate on Scripture, especially the passages that focus on God's love for us (Psalms, Gospels, Paul and John's letters).

Worship: Songs that focus on God's love for you can also be extraordinarily inspiring. Find the best music that expresses this important truth and fill your phone or radio up with the sounds of God's love. Join others in group worship at your local church!

Prayer: Talking *and listening* to God fills the open heart. Find a quiet place to regularly rest in the lavish love of God. Become still enough to hear

His words of grace, love, forgiveness, and delight. He will speak if you are listening.

Messages: Regularly attend a church where the love of God is affirmed in messages and in action. Ask your church office if there are any sermons available for you to on the topic of God's love in Christ. A simple internet search will turn up countless free sermons and teachings on the love of God. For a nominal fee, you can download books, articles, and other lessons on God's love.

The key is for you to find and do the things that open your heart wide to the love of God. His promise is to fill it ... full.

Compassion Fatigue

We've all heard of the problem termed "compassion fatigue" faced by some people involved in draining social work, pastoral care, and dysfunctional relationships. The reality is that the love tank is empty through giving love away without taking enough in. The proverb here isn't so much, "All work and no play makes Jack a dull boy," as it is "All output and no input makes Jack incapable of love." Love has become, or is about to be dried up, not merely tired.

The tragedy of compassion fatigue is that God's love is available for use and is a renewable resource. You can't use up all of God's love because it's *infinite.* More than enough love is available for you to download to cover whatever love needs you encounter. All you must do is take the time to fill up *before* you give it away.

When we love based on human effort, we are saddled with the extraordinary burden of trying to conjure up enough love and find the energy for "doing the loving thing." It doesn't flow from God to us and then through us. Human-powered love saps the life out of us because it is limited and low octane. God's love fills and empowers us with heavenly octane; it is a guaranteed, immeasurable source.[18]

> We are most alive when we are loving and actively giving of
> our lives because we were made to do these things. It is when

we live like this that the Spirit of God moves and acts in and through us in ways that on our own we are not capable of. This is our purpose for living. This is our hope. 'And love does not put us to shame, because God's love has been poured out into our hearts through the Holy Spirit who has been given to us.'[19]

Mother Teresa once said, "We can do no great things, only small things with great love." Likewise Paul could say "I will most gladly spend [myself] and be utterly spent for your souls. If I love you exceedingly, am I to be loved [by you] the less?"[20] Mother Teresa gave of herself with a great love that she received from God. Paul did not fear running out of love. This is why he so freely loved and extended himself to others.

God's love has no shortages. Heaven has no compassion famine. The love manna is available for your daily consumption. God's love is incomprehensibly vast. Once your love tank is filled, it's time to do love.

CONFESSION OF A LOVE HACK
The Pain of Head and Heart

A most unwelcome guest at our house is a migraine. It's the visitor that seems to never go away.

For over thirty-three years, my wife, Laurie, has suffered from migraines. These aren't your typical tension or allergy headaches that recede with a couple of maximum strength acetaminophen and a short nap. Migraines can be debilitating, even with large doses of powerful pharmaceuticals. A dark, quiet room and hours, sometimes days, of fitful sleep can be expected. An occasional trip to the ER isn't out of the question. Whatever was scheduled is postponed or canceled. The rhythm of normal life misses a beat—usually several.

When a migraine calls, no one is happy. Not Laurie. Not our sons. Not her employer. Not her friends. And definitely not her husband.

I hate migraines. In that admission I realize that hate is too nice of a word. I loathe them, abhor them, and cuss them. I despise what they do to my wife, and I detest the unloving person I am when my rhythm of life is syncopated and funky.

When Laurie speaks those dreaded words, "I think I'm getting a headache," my internal world starts reeling. While I know that my chief concern should immediately be for her comfort and well-being, too often my inner rantings reveal that I'm more self-consumed than I'd like to admit. "I'll have to cook dinner." "I'll have to go alone to another church event." "I'll have to tiptoe all day around the house." The awareness of my unlove has reached new depths through reflecting on how poorly I respond to her pain.

Once while mumbling under my breath to God, I said, "I didn't sign up for this." He immediately responded with, "Oh, yes you did. I distinctly recall a commitment you made that included 'in sickness and in health.'" I was busted. I did sign up for loving my wife regardless of how much my life is rearranged by her unwanted and annoying headaches.

I am ashamed at how petty I am. It's embarrassing that I'm so unmoved at her suffering, yet so quick to highlight my inconveniences. I have tried to make life about me, and nothing quite reminds me that I am not in control like a migraine.

Lord, my unlove must pain you far more than a migraine pains my wife. Strengthen me to love her so much that I delight—not despair—in serving her in her times of need.

CHAPTER 6

The Art of Love

"Let all that you do be done in love."
1 Corinthians 16:14

"Do not think that love, in order to be genuine, has to be extraordinary."
Mother Theresa

"The more I think about it, the more I realize there is
nothing more artistic than to love others."
Vincent van Gogh

As the son of a college biology professor, I always had a curiosity about how living things work. How do trees absorb water through their roots deep in the soil and transport it to leaves fifty feet above ground without a pump? How do oversized bumblebees beat their wings so rapidly to make them not only mobile, but surprisingly nimble? How does a cow convert water and grass into milk … or steak? Mm, steak.

While I was in elementary school, my dad occasionally allowed me to wander through the lab storage rooms at the university. There I would find shelves filled with hundreds of jars of amphibians, reptiles, body organs, and other oddities. He allowed me to observe the dissection of a shark, which for a West Texas kid was about like seeing the Loch Ness monster. Later, as a biology student myself, I participated in my fair share of probing the insides of formerly living things—things that were alive at one point but were sacrificed for science.

There are things that dissection can teach. There are things that dissection ruins. It's one thing to see a butterfly fluttering by and alighting on a pincushion flower. It's another fascinating thing to look at the same butterfly or flower under high-powered magnification. The delicate wings or legs of the butterfly or the intricacies of the flower are amazing. When you start dissecting the butterfly or flower something important is lost. Not only must the butterfly and flower be destroyed in the process, but the beauty and mystery of them seem to die as well. So it is with love. Love cannot be dissected without grave consequences. It doesn't bide well under the scalpel, but it will reveal breathtaking beauty through careful observation.

In this chapter I want to give a more detailed picture of love. One of my greatest fears is that in the explanation of love I will butcher it through too much analysis. I am, after all, a love hack. I'm afraid that with the scalpel of scientific investigation I will have a bloodied, dead corpse on my hands instead of a life-giving gift.

Love studied as a scientist or engineer will leave us with a formula or flowchart that makes sense, but it will lack the stuff that makes love come to life in us and through us. The life-giving breath of the Holy Spirit is not a machine that can be duplicated or calibrated. God's love cannot be reduced to a mathematical formula. It cannot be dissected and probed. It can be studied, admired, savored, and meditated upon—and most importantly experienced and done by us.

So with a nod to the value of critical analysis, I hope to be more like a museum docent than a lab tech.[1] A docent helps you see more clearly the nuances of the art you've already been looking at—perhaps a new color, the relationship of one part to another in the frame, or some dramatic touch of the artist's hand that you've previously glossed over.

No one would dare to get a pair of scissors and cut into pieces the masterpieces of Michelangelo, Caravaggio, Monet, or van Gogh just to emphasize the individual elements. Their value stems from the way the parts relate beautifully together as a whole. While you can still focus your attention on smaller details, such as the use of shadows in Caravaggio or the heavy brushstrokes of van Gogh, you do so as it relates to the overall picture. This is the approach we will take with love. Instead of a captivating landscape, think lovescape.

Before we begin our guided tour through love, let me clarify what love we're looking at. Love covers a lot of relationship turf. For example, one may talk about affectionate love between a mother and child, or romantic or erotic love between lovers, or friendship love between close acquaintances. The love we are looking at is broader and deeper than these loves mentioned. Our focus is upon what may be called Christian or sacrificial love.[2] In the original language, the Greek term *agape* is used. *Agape* (or the verb *agapeo*) captures the essence of committed, sacrificial actions for the good of the beloved.

The Big Picture of Love

Imagine *agape* as a large wall mural. I'll draw our attention to different areas of the picture. There is movement by God to us, us to God, and from us to others. Love is not unidirectional; it flows in and out of our lives. Love is also not one-dimensional, focusing on only one aspect such as the will or action. Love involves the complex and synchronized activity of our whole selves. Since I believe that love cannot be exactly arranged in chronological steps, we'll just get started in the middle of the painting.

God is love. Anything we have to say about love must equally be true about God because "God is love."[3] In this sense, God, not us, defines love. We don't merely take human love and multiply it by a million and arrive at God's love. We begin with the known: God is love. Everything else will flow from the reality of God being love as well as expressing love.

Love is revealed. *Agape* is not something that we find on our own, it is something revealed to us. If you want the clearest and most accurate definition of God's love, you must look to Jesus. Our understanding of Jesus is revealed to us through the Bible, and specifically in the Gospels and in the letters of John and Paul. As we read and hear these words, they illicit thoughts, ideas, and images about love (and emotions associated with these thoughts and ideas). Because of the way God created the world and us, love first comes to us from the "outside"—from God to us. "We love because he first loved us."[4] So as we look at the big picture, realize that at all points on the canvas, love is revealed, empowered, and encouraged by God.

Love requires a relationship. An obvious but often overlooked part of the love painting is that love requires an "other." We are not absorbed into some divine harmonic force in the cosmos. Love cannot exist in a relationship vacuum where there is only a singular person. In the Bible there is God in Himself (Trinity), God and us, and us and others. The Song of Songs has a lover and his beloved. It takes two to tango and to love.

Love can be expressed without being reciprocated, but it cannot be experienced unless embraced. You can love someone without their permission or participation; God does this all the time. You can freely and intentionally love a person because of your commitment to be Christlike, regardless of their response to that love. But for love to be really experienced by the beloved, it must be responded to favorably. The lover's joy is not that he or she is being loved back, but that the love given was received and experienced.[5]

So what do we see in our love mural? God in Christ reaches out in love to us; and as we see and receive His love, our love tank gets filled. Out of that fullness, we express love to Him and others. God's love is rooted in His character and identity as God, so our love is to be rooted in our relationship with God and His love being formed in us. Now we, like Him, can love graciously, freely, and sacrificially.

The Love Palette

An expert artist can place five basic colors on her palette and create all other colors from them. By combining the endless varieties of red, blue, yellow, white, and black, any color can be produced. I find this amazing, especially since I'm partially colorblind. Grayscale is my primary color scheme. I'm hoping in heaven I'll have 20/20 color vision to see all of the hues I've missed here on earth.

When you look at a singular act of love, what's involved? How does love work? What are the basic elements to doing something as simple as saying a kind word to a grumpy spouse? I believe that there are five basic, elementary parts that must be present for *agape* love to emerge.[6] As these five colors are mixed on the palette of love and used to paint the love mural, a masterpiece of *agape* will appear, even in quite ordinary situations.

1. Decision: Love does not happen spontaneously and randomly, but because a choice is made. The mural of love shows evidence of resolve, deliberateness, and determination. God chose to love us. Likewise, we simply choose to love as Jesus chose to love us. We easily recognize this in our more intimate relationships. A wedding is a public declaration of a decision to love the other person until separated by death. The marriage vow is an intentional decision; it is not something that we mysteriously drift into against our wills.

If you are going to love at all, you must choose to love.

In the example of loving a grumpy spouse (or child or friend), you begin by choosing to love. You inwardly determine that "I will love him (or her)." This decision may be based on an earlier decision, like a marriage vow, or it may be something fresh and new. Until you decide to love the other person, love won't happen and unlove will.

2. Motive: Motive is that part of the picture that focuses on the noble desire of doing good for the benefit of the other. Here the mural looks like intention, inclination, or disposition. Biblically, the word used most often is compassion. The motive is not selfish desire, but desire for the other's good.

When Jesus saw needy people, he had compassion for them.[7] As a result, he acted in loving ways. He healed, taught, and fed them. When He told the story of the good Samaritan, He says that this man saw the beaten man beside the road and "had compassion" while others deliberately walked past the one suffering.[8] The Samaritan's compassion was expressed in first aid, transportation, help, and provision. Love happened as the heart was moved.

Where does this motivation come from? Ultimately from looking at Christ and having the desire and determination to be like Him. Merely seeing someone in need does not automatically elicit good, noble, compassionate motives. When the grumpy spouse or friend enters the room with sharp words or a hard face, the motivation to love may be quite low. What's the payoff, right? But seeing that Christ has compassion on them and desires to love them means that we too can be compassionate. We love not because the grumpy spouse is loveable, but because Christ moves us with compassion. It's not just that we have to love them, we *want* to love them. God's love changes our motivations by moving us to act compassionately.

It is possible to love with a low motivation so long as you have a high decision, but it is not easy to sustain. Yet when your motive is genuinely for the other person's good, love isn't as hard to do. This is why Jesus said, "my yoke is easy and my burden is light."[9] John said that the commandment to love isn't burdensome.[10] Love isn't drudgery when it's what you want to do.

3. Freedom: For love to be *agape*, it must be a free choice. *Agape* cannot be coerced or manipulated. This is the grace of love. No one forced God to love us; He just freely gave of Himself. If our love is to be like His, then it must be a free choice. Love never happens at the end of a bayonet nor is it enforced through rules and policies. Even when solemn marriage vows are entered into, they cannot be kept without freely choosing to love the other person day after day. Marriage vows are a commitment toward love but don't insure love.

The gift of love must be given without strings attached.[11] "Free love" is not some '60s hippie sexfest, but the reality that love for the other's good is offered unconditionally, meaning we do not hold to a preconceived standard of what their right response should be to our love. Whether or not they change or we are loved back, we freely choose to love.

When the opportunity arises for us to love our grumpy spouse or child, we choose to love them freely. We do it because of God's grace in our lives, not so that the other person will "shape up and fly right." Love is given, not because the other person demands it or deserves it, but because we choose to give it. Our high divorce rates and dead marriages are testaments to the fact that many people simply quit choosing to love. In their minds, the free choice to enter into the marriage becomes the free choice to exit. A word of reminder: Your marriage vows are not a guarantee that your spouse will love you, but your commitment to love him or her. It's your free, uncoerced, and committed choice to love.[12]

4. Knowledge: Let's say you got the first three colors on the palette of love figured out. You are determined to love, you desire to love, and you freely choose to love. The next thing you'll need is the knowledge or understanding of what loving thing to do. For some people, this is easy and obvious. For clueless love hacks like me, this can be taxing and require huge amounts of discernment.

Jesus always did the right loving action for the occasion. He gave sight to the blind, not a plate of bread and fish. He cast out evil spirits in those demonized, but He didn't have them walk on water. Knowledge of the person and his or her need is essential. God loves us perfectly because He knows our real needs and acts out of His goodness for our benefit. Our primary need is for salvation from sin and to know and receive His love. His knowledge of this led Him to send Jesus.

When it comes to loving others, we need to pray for discernment for what is their good. Many times this is clear, like when giving food to the hungry or jobs to the unemployed. But when we look at the daily experiences of life, the lines can get blurry. Take the example of sharing kind words with grumpy people. What, if anything, do you really say? How do you say it? What tone do you use, and what body language do you demonstrate? What actual phrases and sentences do you put together that are genuinely for their good (and not just for defusing them so that they do not explode and make your day miserable)? We may under- or overthink this. It's remarkably easy to assume you know the loving thing—and it's remarkably easy to get it wrong.

So what is the loving thing to do for a grumpy person? I don't know; it depends. There's no one-size-fits-all action in the love closet. The only safe thing to do is pray like crazy for discernment and then ask the important (but now trite) question: "What would Jesus do?" Hold humbly to your answer; it may need revising, but move forward. When you are reasonably sure you know what to do, it's finally time to do love.

Let me pause here long enough to remind you that up to this point no love has actually been expressed. You are poised to love, but you haven't loved yet. One of my personal pitfalls as a love hack is the erroneous assumption that because I've determined to love, I want to love, and because I've got a plan to love that I've actually loved. In my own inflated mind, I'm already a martyr who's done some noble deed. I have loved short, and short love equals unlove. Everything to this point has been happening internally; an experience of and conversation with God and myself. The process can happen in nanoseconds or over the course of several hours. But no one has benefitted from my love. Action is what makes love a gift that benefits others.

5. Action. Now it is time to translate what's going on in our hearts and minds into some bodily action. It is through our actions that we express ourselves to others. You must literally put your body into it.[13] The body is the medium through which all of God's love must pass; as it was for Jesus, so it is with us.

Without actions, there is no love, just love theory. Just as faith without works is dead and just as the body without the spirit is dead, so also love without action is dead.[14]

Imagine loving someone without using your body. You can't talk, write, touch, give, share, kiss, hang out with, Facebook, Tweet, serve, or help. The inert Christian is not the force of world-changing love that God intended. All of the first four colors of love must converge into action. Without action, love with all of its potential is stillborn … a tragic, yet avoidable lapse into unlove. All of the good intended is lost in the internal world of unfulfilled hopes.

If we are to be transformed into loving people who are like Christ, we understand that this begins internally in the grace of God and is continually strengthened by it. But as Dallas Willard says, "Action is indispensable in making the Christian truly a different kind of person …. Failure to act in certain definite ways will guarantee that this transformation does not come to pass."[15] We cannot become loving people without actually doing love.

When we encounter grumpy people, loving actions are the right things to do. By our words (tone and content), body language, attitudes, and tangible actions, we humbly extend ourselves to them for their good. This may mean giving them time off for a nap or a moment of solitude, offering an encouraging word or an attentive ear, or inviting them into some activity to distract them from whatever led to their sour mood. But make no mistake, loving them requires an action on your part; you must engage them. Take it from one love hack to another, responding to their grumpiness with self-justified defensiveness or apathy is a death sentence.

One of the harshest realities that contemporary believers avoid is the connection between identity/character and actions. Biblically, our actions reveal our character. God does loving things because He is love. His inner life and outer actions are seamlessly united. We, however, live under the illusion that we can be loving, holy, and God's child without any effect on the way we live. We are most truthfully known through our actions.[16]

Our actions are the best indicators of our true beliefs, not the abstract and counterfeit ones we spout off in our public professions. No place is this more evident than in love.

According to John, it is impossible to confess love for God without the tangible evidence of love for others.[17] By our actions toward others, our love for God is either expressed or denied.

It won't take long in doing love that you'll realize that your body seems to have a mind all its own. Sin has already worked its way into the fabric of your body parts. Your facial expressions and vocal tones are harsh or flat. Your words are distorted on the way out of your mouth. Your pulse quickens and your blood pressure shoots up when you don't get your way. What we think should be obvious and clear to others is overlooked or undervalued. Your noble intentions and loving ideas melt into actions so small and indiscernible that even you can't see them in hindsight. Our attempts at love vaporize into nothingness. The habit of love cannot be learned in a six-hour seminar. God's classroom on *agape* is for life.

All five colors on the love palette are used in creating the art of love. As you can see, a simple act of love involves many interdependent parts within you. "Do love" is far more than a futile exercise in behavior modification because it involves *all* of you. But one part that I've intentionally been silent about until now is that of your feelings or emotions. Feelings or emotions are not required to love someone. We are never commanded in Scripture to "*feel* love for another," but simply to *do love*. When we chase the feeling of love or refuse to act lovingly until we feel like it, we will eventually cease to love altogether. Loving actions are indispensable; loving feelings are optional.[18]

Just because you use all five colors on the love palette doesn't mean all will turn out well. Jesus loved perfectly and was murdered for it. His call for us to take up the cross and follow Him isn't a siren's song to an easy road. Love will be costly, but we willingly pay the price.

When you love another person for their good, you are rewarded with the fact that *love is God's will*. They may not have known about your loving action or responded as you would have wished. Your act of love may seem to have little effect on them or even your life in particular. You may even be surprised that doing love isn't always an enjoyable experience—that you really don't feel any better for doing it. The value of love is first and foremost centered on what is given away, not on what is personally gained.[19] *Agape* is radically other-focused.

When we learn to love with our bodies, we will find a certain initial awkwardness. Expect it. Many may quit with their first few attempts at love because it's so uncomfortable or unrewarded. The love flywheel is just gaining momentum. The process of uprooting the persistent weeds of selfishness already present in our bodies and planting and cultivating a lifestyle of love is not quick or easy. It's a work that requires you to be fully engaged with God and His grace over a long time. But change will come! There's hope for love hacks! The Spirit of Jesus will lead us (if we'll be led) into an ever-increasing life of love to the degree that our bodily actions are habitually and even unconsciously loving to others.

Hopefully you've grown to appreciate the love mural that God presents to us. It's huge, beautiful, and beyond compare. His love for us uses all of the colors on the love palette, and calls for us to do the same. Now it is time for us to pick up the brush, imitate the Master, and paint pictures of love with our lives.

CONFESSION OF A LOVE HACK
The Legalism of Unlove

Ted moved from Fallbrook, California, to Abilene, Texas, right before his senior year of high school. His father, a former officer in the Marines, relocated due to his new job. For Ted, it was a forced march in a direction he didn't want to go. He was a laid-back, West Coast surfer now in the desert flatlands of West Texas. Boots, not sandals, were the footwear of choice.

We met on the high school swim team; he had water polo experience and was a strong swimmer. With his easygoing style and love for classic rock, he quickly made a place for himself on the roster.

Ted and I shared some incredibly fun times, many of them bordering on dangerous stupidity. As teenage guys, our frontal lobes of good judgment were greatly underdeveloped. On one swim team tournament, we snuck out of the bathroom window of our hotel room and illegally bluffed our way into a honky-tonk. I never laughed as hard as I did watching Ted attempt the Texas two-step. With his California one-step, tennis shoes, and Hawaiian shirt, he didn't exactly blend in with the locals.

Over the course of the year, I slowly realized how weak an influence I was on Ted. I was a Christian, or so I professed—obviously, my lifestyle smacked of hypocrisy. My spiritual light was dim and my moral salt was insipid. My Sunday life was nothing like the rest of my week.

The week after high school graduation, I finally pushed through my guilt, gave him a Bible, and wrote him a letter about trusting in Jesus. To my surprise, he soon accepted Christ. We were now brothers in the Lord!

In the fall, he attended Texas Tech University, a large state school, while I went to Hardin-Simmons University, a small Baptist one. He lived with license; I embraced legalism. After one semester, he transferred to Hardin-Simmons and became my roommate.

Our close proximity to each other erupted in occasional clashes. My unlove manifested itself in high standards of self-righteousness that I imposed on Ted. I determinedly and arrogantly tried to form him into my image. I was blind to my own inconsistencies while openly condemning his. I tried to use anger and open disapproval to corral him. He rightly bucked up against my narrow-mindedness.

A relational drift started—nothing hostile, just a slow fade. He went his way, and I mine. We occasionally reminisced about old times together, but there remains to this day an unresolved parting that is largely the result of my unloving attempts to control him—not for his good per se, but to feel better about my own failures and to impress a girlfriend with my spirituality. I was a judgmental love hack.

Unlove erodes relationships, even those between close friends.

Dear Jesus, please strip off the veneer of my false spirituality that suffocates real love. May I simply love people as you do—without legalism, condemnation, or coercion.

CHAPTER 7

Swimming in Love

"Above all, keep loving one another earnestly."
1 Peter 4:8a

"I hear, I forget.
I see, I remember.
I do, I understand."
African Proverb

Ama Deum et fac quod vis.
[Love, and do as you like.]
St. Augustine

I love water—not just the drinking kind, but also the fun kind.

For as long as I can remember, I've swum, waded, splashed, and dived in pools, lakes, rivers, and oceans. I've fished, sailed, canoed, kayaked, bodysurfed, skied, snorkeled, jumped off of cliffs, and even panned for gold in water. I've raced on swim teams and in triathlons. I've lifeguarded numerous summers. My "bucket list" includes watery feats of valor and stupidity.[1] Even now the smell of a salty ocean, an earthy lake, or a chlorinated pool will dredge up all kinds of memories for me. Much of my life can be chronicled in water.

As a starving college and grad school student, I earned cash by teaching swim lessons. I would take kids (some as young as eighteen months) and teach them how to hold their breath, kick, swim, and float while in the water. After two weeks, they'd jump off the side of the pool or diving board and swim back to safety. After years of giving instructions, I can say confidently that people cannot really learn to swim without getting into the water. However much they can grasp the concepts of aquatic propulsion from a book or off the Internet, until they get in the water and feel it physically, they simply won't know how to swim.

But getting a water-shy kid into the pool isn't easy. Swimming requires being *in* the water. You must get wet, not just your big toe or even from the knees down, but all of you. Terrified newbies will inch to the edge of the pool, sometimes scooting on their rears. They go through a whole gamut of bodily gyrations. They may cry, scream, bargain, or become rigid as an oak board or as lively as an alley cat tossed in the tub. They'll dig their heels into solid concrete if you try to drag them in. They want assurances of the close and physical kind. If you give them your hand, they're likely to crawl up your arm to the top of your head. They sputter. They manipulate. They divert attention. They will do whatever it takes to avoid the water and learn to swim—until they learn how to swim, then you can't get them out.

Love is like this. At some point we have to peel ourselves away from the props of books and intellectual knowledge, pry our toes off the edge of the selfish or familiar, and jump into life and love others. *Love is learned in the act of doing it.* In the same way we become comfortable and adept in the water, so too, do we enter into the messy and scary world of relationships; we learn love by the very act of loving.[2] But once you start getting the hang of it, you'll not want to live any other way.

"Action Trumps Everything"

Entrepreneurial guru Len Schlesinger believes that three key words can guide most of our daily lives and serve as a useful business model: act, learn, repeat.[3] Take action, evaluate that action, and then immediately take action again. This is how we learned to walk and talk as toddlers, even after weeks of repeated failures. When this action-oriented principle is guided by the words and example of Christ, love *will* happen.

Many people enter into the paralysis of analysis when it comes to the things of God, especially love. They want to make sure that they "get it right." Guess what? Let me relieve you of this burden; in most situations, you won't get it 100 percent right. What's more, 80 percent of right (loving) actions are always better than 0 percent of no actions. Even 30 percent is good. *Any* percentage of love is better than zero percent. Thinking about love doesn't actually change anything or anyone's life. Love in action does. *Inaction equals unlove.*

This same idea is echoed by Clare de Graaf in his book, *The 10 Second Rule.* He says, "Just do the next thing you're reasonably certain Jesus wants you to do (and commit to it immediately—in the next 10 seconds—before you change your mind)."[4] When applied to love, we are to do whatever loving action we are reasonably certain Jesus wants us to do in the next ten seconds. This model doesn't get gummed up with absolute certainty of what to do, just do what you're reasonably certain Jesus wants you to do. Immediate action trumps. As Seth Godin says, "Soon is not as good as now."[5] Love immediately, evaluate, and repeat.

My wife Laurie suffers from chronic migraines. When she is in the agony of intense pain, our goal is to find the fastest way, if possible, to alleviate her suffering. Both she and I work together in trying to find the best relief given the circumstances. This usually means prescription medicine and rest, but may include other things such as creating a dark, quiet, cool room or taking a special combination of over-the-counter drugs that she's found to be helpful. Occasionally a migraine leads to lengthy bouts of nausea and dehydration that require an IV to get her back on track. When the migraine is first sensed, we spring into action. Many times, we do not find the best solution the first time, but this process of act–evaluate–repeat eventually lands on the best plan for relief.

By guiding our actions with the words of Christ, we will find plenty of actions to immediately take. Jesus Himself was very action-oriented in both His teachings and example. The spiritual word for this is *obedience.* Doing the Father's will is obedience; and obedience (action) is how we demonstrate love for God and others. Jesus said it plainly, "If you love me, you will keep my commandments."[6] He isn't giving us a guilt trip to emotionally manipulate us into obedience. He's simply stating the facts, as if to say that you can't do algebra until you understand the multiplication tables. It's not that you can't try to do algebra, but that regardless of your efforts, you won't be successful. In order for us to love Jesus, we must demonstrate that love through obedient actions.

The One-Anothers

If we're trying to immediately love according to the ways of Jesus, what are we supposed to be doing? Fortunately we have an answer to this question. I believe that the key to understanding how to love people is contained in the thirty-seven "one another" passages in the New Testament. These phrases give a specific action (with a presumed loving attitude), often in the command form, as a way of loving each other. Some of them have significant overlap; but taken together, we have a comprehensive way of loving each other. These commands are much broader in scope than our marriages, friendships, or even Christian circles. They tell us how to relate to all people in a Christlike way. The "one-anothers" refer to anyone who is not you—literally whoever is "an other" person.

I want to be clear here. The one-anothers are not just a biblical veneer to rehash Gary Chapman's well-known five love languages.[7] While I certainly have benefited from Chapman's work on helping people understand their inclination toward expressing love in certain ways, the one-another approach to love is distinctive. Pragmatically, Chapman may be right that we have tendencies to certain ways of loving and receiving love; but biblically we are not afforded the luxury of fixating on a personal favorite "language," and we justifiably neglect other ways as "that's just not my thing." Although Chapman's approach encourages us to understand how to love others differently from the way we might prefer to receive love, too often we downgrade it a mantra for selfishness: "How do *I* want to receive love? How do *I* give love?"[8]

I've heard and experienced my fair share of comments using this approach: "Love me this way, not that way" or "Hey, I loved you the way you wanted, what's the problem now?" This line of thinking may help in certain relationships, but as a whole it falls painfully short of the biblical mandate to love all people, whether it's your love language or not. When we uncritically adopt this cafeteria approach, we ultimately get to pick and choose how we want to love and receive love from others. This places unlove in sheep's clothing.

I've arranged the one-anothers into seven categories that seem to follow a natural alignment.[9]

1. Love is kind.
2. Love is humble.
3. Love serves.
4. Love cares.
5. Love welcomes.
6. Love speaks truth.
7. Love values the relationship.

Each of these is to be *done* by all believers, no exceptions. Regardless of one's spiritual gifts and personality type, clear biblical commands should be followed. Granted, some of these commands will be easier than others, but all should be relentlessly pursued. They guide and define how we are to treat all people. Now let's look at each category and the specific one-anothers that apply.

1. Love is Kind.
"Love one another." (John 13:34; 15:12, 17)
"Love one another with brotherly affection." (Rom. 12:10)
"Be kind to one another." (Eph. 4:32)
"Be tenderhearted." (Eph. 4:32)
"Stir up one another to love." (Heb. 10:24)

One of the basic definitions of love in 1 Corinthians 13 is "love is kind." Kindness is how love treats people; it's the etiquette of love. Kindness includes what is done as well as how it is done. Kindness communicates value to the other person.[10] When you have genuine regard for the needs of others and treat them with sensitivity, you are being kind and loving.

Imagine that you're in a long line at the local grocery. The person checking out at the register has a thick envelope of coupons that she's rifling through. The cashier seems slow and incompetent. The lady in front of you is trying to corral three young children while keeping her place in line. What's your reaction? Deep sighs? Rolling your eyes at the people behind you? Clenching your jaw as you stare a hole through your melting ice cream? Tweeting your friends about your shopping woes to vent your frustration and curry a little empathy? Does love toward the people around you even enter your mind? What would kind and compassionate actions look like in this scenario?

It may sound redundant to say that "love is loving," but Jesus' repeated words to "love one another" is the foundational commandment for all expressions of love. He later redefines this love not as loving your neighbor as yourself, which may be quite distorted and self-centered, but to love others "as I have loved you." *Agapeo* is the chosen word here; Jesus loves us sacrificially and expects *agape* to be our standard for loving others. The "brotherly affection" passage in Romans 12:10 uses two separate Greek words for love: *philos* and *storge*—the love between friends and familial love, respectively. We are to treat other people as friends and family members.

The call in Hebrews 10:24 to "stir up one another to love" is a love oddity. The picture here is spurring a slow horse or goading a stubborn mule. The idea of irritating each other in such a way as to move the other person to loving actions sounds like a recipe for relational carnage. If I may give some advice here: prod gently, but don't puncture. This command must be delicately applied or else it becomes a license for unlove in the name of Jesus. Consider well your words and tone when dealing with sensitive people; what may be an acceptable goad to a driven Type A person may be lethal to someone else. Remember, the focus here is to kindly poke without inflicting damage.

2. Love is Humble.
"Clothe yourselves with humility toward one another."
(1 Peter 5:5, NIV)
"In humility count others more significant than yourselves."
(Phil. 2:3)
"Submit to one another." (Eph. 5:21, NIV)
"Honor one another above yourselves." (Rom. 12:10, NIV)
Do not "be inflated with pride." (1 Cor. 4:6, HCSB)

Humility is one of those often-misunderstood words, as if real spirituality confesses, "Worm am I" to the glory of God. Humble people don't necessarily think poorly of themselves, they just think of themselves less because they are thinking of others more. First Corinthians 13:5 says that love "does not insist on its own way." Because the nature of love is to act for the good of the other, it is not consumed with making sure that one's personal needs are the centerpiece. Humble people express love because they put the needs and preferences of others above their own. Humility isn't just what you don't do, where you sit by quietly and idly and let others have their own way. Humility actively pursues the good of others; you are *for them*. Humble love actively seeks to honor the other person above the self through tangible actions.

To me, nothing is more humbling than to be a short-term missionary in an impoverished or developing nation. Once, while in Cuba, a pastor invited me to his home and offered me a huge portion of the best food he had. At that time, Cuba enforced a strict food-rationing program. As I ate, I know that he was not thinking about himself or even his family, but simply how he could demonstrate appreciation and honor to someone who had traveled to encourage him and his ministry. This man, his family, and his neighbors needed this food far more than I did. But it was offered with such sincere humility and grace that I ate everything placed in front of me, fried plantains and all.

Graciously deferring to others may take the form of letting them hold the TV remote, letting their plans or ideas move the company forward instead of yours, eating their favorite food instead of insisting on yours, or simply listening well without interruptions. Insisting on our own way is just one way that unlove rears its ugly head. When in doubt about which loving action to take, choose the path that will require the most humility.

3. Love Serves.
"Through love serve one another." (Gal. 5:13)
"Bear one another's burdens." (Gal. 6:2)
"Each one should use whatever gift he has received to serve others." (1 Peter 4:10, NIV)
"Contribute to the needs of the saints." (Rom. 12:13)
"Wash one another's feet." (John 13:14)

Action is easily seen in service. Here, love sees and meets other people's needs. It can be as simple as cooking a meal, cleaning a room, or fixing a car. Because 1 Peter 4:10 includes using your spiritual gift as the way that you serve others, this opens up the possibilities for showing love in several different ways—giving, encouraging, teaching, leading, building something, and so on.

For service to be love, it must be for the benefit of the other person. The mom who cleans her son's room because she can't stand the messiness any longer may be motivated by her own obsessive need for cleanliness, not the good of her son. Service is offered for the recipient's good, not your own neediness. Jesus washed the disciples' feet, not to meet some personal emotional need of His own, but because their feet were dirty and it was ultimately for their benefit to learn about humble service through Him.

Sotea is a Cambodian believer with a high capacity to love through serving. Her husband is an unbeliever who works in the military, so all of her service to others receives little or no support from the home. At conferences for church leaders, she is the lead chef in the kitchen. I say chef because her food is too delicious to come from a mere cook. She joyfully and tirelessly works from predawn until sunset preparing and cooking meat, rice, and vegetables on wood stoves with enormous woks. Through her loving service, she caters to the needs of these church leaders and special guests and makes them feel valued. Her service is love in action.

Service opportunities generally provide the clearest activities that are beneficial to another person vs. beneficial to the self. Many cities and churches have food pantries and soup lines that provide structured ways to serve others in love. Almost every church, shelter, or community center has lists of menial jobs that need to be done in love to help minister to needy people. Do love means service.

4. Love Cares.
"Care for one another." (1 Cor. 12:25)
"Pray for one another." (James 5:16)
"Rejoice with those who rejoice." (Rom. 12:15)
"Weep with those who weep." (Rom. 12:15)
"Comfort one another." (2 Cor. 13:11)
"Wait for one another." (1 Cor. 11:33)

Love seeks to connect with people through prayer, empathy, comfort, and patience. When others are hurting, we enter into their hurt. When they are thrilled about something good that's come into their lives, we celebrate with them. When they are hurting, grieving, or are confused, we comfort. We love and care for others when we put some real skin in the game.[11] You can't love and care without getting directly involved in their lives.

My wife has astutely observed that of all the one-anothers listed here, the real litmus test of love is rejoicing with one another. Believers will quickly pray or grieve over someone who is genuinely hurting, weeping, or experiencing a hardship. Yet when someone has a genuine blessing to share, Christians often become jealous, feeling entitled to a little heavenly goodness themselves. Sometimes they go the route of "upping"—whatever blessing you shared, theirs is bigger. Why is it so hard for us to be happy for the good experienced by someone else? Our lack of joy for the blessings of others says more about the condition of our hearts than our ability to weep when they hurt.

My own personal struggle is with the simple command to "wait for one another." To wait is to be patient; and "love is patient." We keep pace with the ones we love most. Love does not drive the beloved along like an Eskimo mushes dogs or lag behind the beloved with a sullen attitude. My problem is that I prefer to keep pace with me. Small talk is for those with time, not for me. Whether I'm jogging with a running partner, getting ready for an event with my wife, sitting in a leadership meeting, or walking through a mall, I'm eaten up with what John Ortberg calls the hurry sickness.

> The most serious sign of hurry sickness is a diminished capacity to love. Love and hurry are fundamentally incompatible. Love always takes time, and time is the one thing hurried people don't have … Hurried people cannot love.[12]

Doing love takes time … patient, unhurried time. One of my growth edges in learning to love is shopping for clothes with my wife. My caveman approach to shopping is walk in, get what I want within three minutes, and exit the store. It's taken me twenty-five years of marriage to realize that Laurie enjoys just looking, thinking, dreaming, redesigning, and touching fabrics when she shops. She's not there necessarily to buy, but to experience new things. I've actually gotten to the point where I don't mind following her wanderings around a store or mall (as long as it doesn't last more than three hours). Love cares enough to go the pace of the beloved.

5. Love Welcomes.
"Welcome one another." (Rom. 15:7)
"Show hospitality to one another." (1 Peter 4:9)
"Greet one another." (Rom. 16:16)
"Fellowship with one another." (1 John 1:7)
"Let us not pass judgment on one another." (Rom. 14:13)

This aspect of love focuses on how we respond to others when they come into our presence. Love welcomes them with acceptance, open arms, and without judgment. The image of the father running to and embracing the prodigal son should be our normal response to those around us. When you look at the composite picture of how Jesus interacted with the people around Him, we clearly see one who welcomed others graciously.

Let me challenge you through a short, mental exercise based on Romans 15:7, "Welcome one another as Christ has welcomed you." Visualize what it looks like for Jesus to receive you into His presence. What are His facial expressions—His body language—His words? What does He do to convey to you how much He loves you? In the same way that Jesus receives you into His presence, this is how we are to receive one another.

What I believe that Jesus envisions here is not simply a well-ordered and well-mannered welcome team at the local church, where cars are parked and bulletins are handed out by smiling, cheerful people. Even Walmart has greeters; can't we do better than that? When love welcomes others, it does so seven days a week both privately and publicly. Love genuinely is glad to see others and receives them into one's personal favor—whether they are spouses, children, coworkers, or others completely unknown. Instead of dodging one another in grocery aisles, ignoring the new person sitting alone in church, or marginalizing someone because of a full friendship quota, love reaches out and welcomes others in to a genuine nonjudgmental relationship.

6. Love Speaks Truth.

"Instruct one another." (Rom. 15:14)

"Teaching and admonishing one another." (Col. 3:16)

"Addressing one another." (Eph. 5:19)

"Confess your sins to one another." (James 5:16)

"Encourage one another." (1 Thess. 5:11)

Love includes communication: what we say and how we say it. Too often, the command to speak the truth is misinterpreted as a license to be harsh and cruel. We are instructed to "speak the truth in love."[13] Truth is the content; lovingly or kindly is how it is delivered. Love "rejoices with the truth."[14] When truth is spoken with the absence of love, it becomes a destructive weapon that slashes or bludgeons others. Truth is to be shared with others in a life-giving way. Unlove turns truth that heals into mere knowledge that kills. When we violate the "in love" part of speaking truth, whatever we may say becomes untruth. Even when Jesus confronted the Pharisees with His seven woes,[15] He authoritatively spoke with genuine love. His heart's desire was their repentance to spiritual life, not their condemnation to eternal death.

When love speaks, teaches, or encourages others, it does not do so condescendingly or smugly. Talking is not simply an opportunity to air one's personal opinion or expertise. Humility and grace guard the mouth. Even in the confession of our sins to others, we truthfully speak about our shortcomings in a way that doesn't make the moment about us. Confession keeps the other person informed of who we really are so that we don't misrepresent or overvalue ourselves.

As a pastor, I have experienced the double edge of truth. I have preached or counseled with great compassion and empathy while speaking truth. It's a flow of spiritual power that's quite amazing. I have also spoken words of truth without love. These words are flat and uninspiring. People exit the building quickly afterwards; counseling sessions become awkward and forced. No one lingers where truth and unlove meet. Love is what gives passion and life to our words. Be careful to always speak the truth in love *after* careful prayer and consideration. Remember we are to be quick to listen and slow to speak.[16]

7. Love Values the Relationship.
"Live in harmony with one another." (Rom. 12:16)
"Agree with one another." (2 Cor. 13:11)
"Forgiving each other." (Eph. 4:32; Col. 3:13)
"Bearing with one another." (Col. 3:13)
"Do not grumble against one another." (James 5:9)
"Do not speak evil against one another." (James 4:11)

We've all heard the joke that life would be easy, if it weren't for all the other people.[17] The only problem, of course, is that people are an inevitable and unavoidable part of life: family, neighbors, friends, coworkers, students, teachers, and churches, crowds at football games and on the freeway. People, people everywhere! People, however, are ultimately not the problem. It's the people who are different from us that are the problem, and that's pretty much everyone else on the planet. *Every* relationship has a certain amount of built-in friction. Love values the relationship by greasing the relationship friction through forgiveness, deference, and positive talk.

Love does not allow offenses, snide comments, or annoying personality habits to ruin the relationship. Because relationships are valued, people aren't disposable. Love chooses to forgive and bear with the other person's shortcomings while humbly acknowledging one's own. Love actively seeks to build bridges and extend the olive branch of peace. Love does not speak unbecomingly of the other person, even if what is said is true. Relationships are protected by the refusal to speak or hear evil of others.

When I am giving premarital advice, I always cover three important verses of Scripture: "Speak the truth in love" (Eph. 4:15), "Be quick to hear, slow to speak, and slow to anger" (James 1:19), and "Forgiving each other as God in Christ forgave you" (Eph. 4:32). My logic is that if we can get communication right, increase good listening, minimize anger, and establish gracious forgiveness as the norm, most marriages will last. After twenty-five years of marriage and countless hours of counseling with couples, I now believe that of these three verses, the most important one is on forgiveness. Offenses, hurts, and miscommunications will happen regardless of how diligently you follow good rules of communication. In the trenches of life, it is forgiveness that keeps relationships intact. Without it, intolerant bitterness consumes us. One of the most important acts of love is to value the relationship so much that you forgive offenses and maintain a door of openness to the other person.

Love opens the door for God's life to flow into us, and through us into others. "Failure to love others as Jesus loves us … chokes off the flow of the eternal kind of life that our whole human system cries out for."[18] When John says, "The one who does not love abides in death," he was speaking of unlove broadly, not hate alone. "The mere absence of love is deadly."[19] When we value relationships so much that we forgive, avoid slander and gossip, and remain open and available to the other person, God's life and love will pour through us.

Is Perfect Possible?

If a person loves from the heart according to these one-another passages, I believe that his or her love will be strong and mature. In 1 John 4, three references are made regarding a perfect or fully mature love.[20] A few years back as a seasoned love hack, I thought that "perfect love" was impossible. How could someone like me become a perfect lover? Yet this is what we are called to—a mature, complete, or perfect love. Perfect here does not mean being flawless, but complete and mature, like a plant that has grown to the point of bearing viable fruit.

Perfect love is not a dream or a fantasy, but a reality that Jesus intends for His followers to experience. The only time we are told to "be perfect" in the Bible is in Matthew 5:48 in the context of loving like God. By consistently following the tangible actions of the one another passages in the New Testament, mature love is not only a possibility, but will become a reality in time. The one-anothers are our blueprint for mature love.

Therapy is a tricky word. It can refer to physical therapy, where the body recaptures a previous range of motion, increases in strength, or learns a new skill. Psychological therapy may mean talking with a counselor privately or in a group setting about how to improve your patterns of relating to others. Spiritual therapy is learning how to unlearn our sinful patterns and replace them with Christlike patterns in our thoughts, desires, and actions. Regardless of what type of therapy you're looking at, the key is repetition of the desired thoughts and behavior.

Learning to love will be a lot like therapy—possibly painful at first as you use love muscles that you've ignored or that have atrophied. But over time, those muscles will become flexible and strong. Like all routine bodily motions, the ideal is when action becomes unconscious—when you don't have to think about it, you just love because that's who you've become by the grace of God. Mature, Christlike love is able to move through the full range of motions given to us in the one-anothers.

We learn to walk, talk, swim, and virtually everything else by the simple method of act, evaluate, repeat. The same method works with love: do the one-anothers, evaluate, and repeat immediately. Don't hesitate; just jump in … the water's fine.

CONFESSION OF A LOVE HACK
Too Late for Love

It wasn't her fault.

Really it wasn't. That my itinerary had been rescheduled for an hour after my original departure time. Or that the plane was now fifty-five minutes later still. That my standard-sized carry-on wouldn't fit in the tiny overhead compartments of the commuter plane. That it looked as if I wouldn't make my connecting flight to London. That my hopes and plans were turned upside down.

I felt trapped emotionally and could feel the irritation and frustration rise. I had just enough presence of mind to not vent on my wife. Instead, I directed my anger at the flight attendant. My impatience did not come out with a loud screaming rant, but with a low-grade seething at her and at all that her airline company represented. She and her airline were ruining my vacation merely hours into it!

About midflight and after several checks in my spirit by God and a few "it's going to be okay" looks from my wife, I tried to shift gears. They felt stuck. The commitment to my agenda had blinded me to how my actions were impatient, self-serving, and unloving. I had just hacked loved again. Just love, Andrew. Do love.

I began to say "please" and "thank you" again. I didn't feel as resentful when the flight attendant kept bumping into my shoulder when she passed. I even asked her nicely if there was any way she could check to see if our connecting flight to London had left or been delayed. Her response for me to wait until we landed and use my smartphone to check online gave me more of a sense of disbelief than ire. Perhaps my unlove had been showing more vividly than I imagined.

It wasn't her fault for the circumstances beyond her control. It was my fault for the unloving attitude and actions. I'm a love hack. Rearrange my schedule for a few minutes and you'll see.

Lord, save others from my self-serving agenda. May I love others as you do.

CHAPTER 8

Love Hurts

"By this we know love, that he laid down his life for us,
and we ought to lay down our lives for the brothers."
1 John 3:16

"To be able to say how much you love is to love but little."
Petrarch

"The only place outside of Heaven where you can be perfectly safe
from all the dangers and perturbations of love is Hell."
C.S. Lewis

*I*t's happened innumerable times before. By the water cooler in the office or on the back patio at a party, some guy complains about his sore back or his gimpy knee. This spawns further discussion among the guys of old sports injuries. Soon the conversation moves on to broken bones, stitches, and car accidents as each man "ups" the previous story with more gruesome details and unthinkable pain. For men, scars are cool. Endured pain is studly.

Then it happens—a woman enters the conversation. With a toss of her hair and a roll of her eyes, she says those dreaded words that suck the air right out of space. "Yeah, try having a baby." Then mothers materialize out of the walls and turn on the men like a pack of ravenous wolves, wild-eyed and foaming at the mouth. "You don't know the pain of having a baby." Graphic illustrations of large pieces of fruit passing through a wedding ring have the men squeamishly shifting their weight, coughing dryly, and staring blankly at the floor. They are silenced into submission.

We men know that even if we were to catch our foot in a lawnmower and then fall into a vat of lemon juice, it still wouldn't hold a candle to childbirth. The pain of childbirth is the ultimate trump card that mothers will forever hold over their sons and husbands. Forever. Until Jesus comes back.

What mothers go through in pregnancy and birth is nothing short of phenomenal. They sacrifice their bodies in the act of bringing a new life into the world. Their gift of bearing a child comes at a high cost, and their bodies are never quite the same again. A hundred "Mother's Days" a year still couldn't capture all of the honor due to loving mothers. About the only thing able to arrest both men and women's natural tendency to exalt our pain and suffering is for us to look collectively at the passion and death of Jesus Christ. At the foot of the cross, we all see love being expressed in the ultimate way and through the ultimate price.

"Greater Love"

Hours before His death, Jesus shared these profound words with His closest followers:

> This is my commandment, that you love one another as I have loved you. Greater love has no one than this, that someone lay down his life for his friends. (John 15:12–13)

Words like these would be deceptively hollow if they were not backed up by actions. Jesus pointed to His track-record of love to these men, and then ahead to the cross when He would literally lay down His life for them. His whole life and death were an example of sacrificial love.

Jesus' "greater love" was painful. He willingly died for you as an expression of God's love. All of the beatings, ridicule, indignities, sheer agony, and loss of blood as well as the spiritual and psychological stress He endured were enormous. His death on our behalf was the definitive answer to the question, "Does God love me?" Through Jesus on the cross, God demonstrated His love to people just like us.[1] All that stood against us—sin, death, hell, and Satan—were thrown at Jesus unmercifully.

Since love is an intentional action for the good of others, there is no greater love than Christ's because of its greatest good to the greatest number of people. Jesus died to provide the forgiveness of sins and eternal life to every single person who would believe in Him. Through the gift of His life, He offered a new power for living. No one else in the world has ever loved so deeply and widely.

Through His death, Jesus teaches us about *agape's* incredible capacity to suffer. Genuine love is able to endure much pain, hurt, offenses, and personal sacrifice. A love unwilling to suffer is suspect. A fair-weather friend isn't so friendly after all. When the threshold of suffering is crossed, love theorists and love practitioners separate. Theorists will cheer for love as long as the price tag is low and investment is short. Practitioners may not cheer like teenage girls, but they will endure during difficult times.[2]

Let me be crystal clear here. Love does not equal spiritual masochism, which is a self-centered perversion. Loving people do not seek to suffer nor do they find pleasure in suffering. Their goal is merely to love, and if the good they render to the other requires suffering, they willingly endure it. Masochists seek and "enjoy" suffering, not for the good of others, but for self-fulfillment. Lovers suffer for others, as needed. Masochists suffer for themselves, as desired. By definition, masochism cannot be love because it doesn't exists for the good of another person.

As we seek to become "greater love" people, there's no shortcut on the love flywheel. We must see the love of Jesus with incredible clarity and insight. We must experience His love in a personal and transformative way. We must commit to becoming like Him; sacrificial love is intentional. We must also do love in real, tangible ways that follow His example, even if it requires us to sacrifice greatly. We are called to lay down our lives for others, but what does this really mean?

The Question of Love

For years I've been fascinated by the lives (and deaths) of martyrs. I've read books and accounts, modern and ancient, of believers who remained faithful to Christ when the fires of persecution were turned up. Once in Rome, I spent an afternoon in an offbeat church called St. Stephen's Rotunda. There I studied the thirty-four ancient frescos of various tortures and martyrdoms from the early church. What motivated these believers to endure boiling oil, being torn apart by wild animals, having body parts crushed or hacked off, or being burned at the stake? Sheer will power or mass delusion cannot explain this level of commitment to Jesus Christ. Only love could inspire such devotion.[3]

I've heard many people say that they could never be a martyr because their threshold for pain is incredibly low. I no longer think that this is the issue. I'm pretty sure that many people who have suffered and even died for Christ were wienies like the rest of us. What they lacked in pain tolerance, they made up for in love. Immense love for God and His people—along with God's unique grace given to strengthen a person during especially difficult times of persecution— carried them through their times of trials. Fortunately for us, the sacrificial love that we're called to exemplify will not likely require martyrdom, but simple and tangible acts of love to others.

Simon Peter is one of my favorite biblical characters. I can relate to his bias to action, often without a well-thought-out plan. His confessions and commitments often outran his heart. Peter was the first inductee into the Love Hack Hall of Fame. He promises undying faithfulness to Jesus, and then hours later denied Him before a servant girl in the shadows of predawn. Peter no doubt loved Jesus, but his love was incomplete and immature.

After His resurrection, Jesus confronts Peter about the quality of his love in John 22. Jesus asked a penetrating question that probes the hearts of us all. "Do you really love Me?"

> When they had finished breakfast, Jesus said to Simon Peter, "Simon, son of John, do you love [*agapeo*] me more than these?" He said to him, "Yes, Lord; you know that I love [*phileo*] you." He said to him, "Feed my lambs." He said to him a second time, "Simon, son of John, do you love [*agapeo*] me?" He said to him, "Yes, Lord; you know that I love [*phileo*] you." He said to him, "Tend my sheep." He said to him the third time, "Simon, son of John, do you love [*phileo*] me?" Peter was grieved because he said to him the third time, "Do you love [*phileo*] me?" and he

said to him, "Lord, you know everything; you know that I love [*phileo*] you." Jesus said to him, "Feed my sheep. Truly, truly, I say to you, when you were young, you used to dress yourself and walk wherever you wanted, but when you are old, you will stretch out your hands, and another will dress you and carry you where you do not want to go." (This he said to show by what kind of death he was to glorify God.) And after saying this he said to him, "Follow me." (John 22:15–19)[4]

Peter, who earlier had confidently committed himself to die for Jesus, was now not so assertive of his love. Peter avowed friendship love (*phileo*), but wasn't so cocky as to confess sacrificial love (*agapeo*). He had already demonstrated how easily he could buckle under pressure. Jesus knew that *agape* was the key to Peter enduring future trials and persecutions; friendship love simply wouldn't have the horsepower. Instead of condemning Peter as a hopeless love hack, Jesus called him into a greater and deeper love that would come with time. Jesus prophesied that Peter would in fact die a martyr's death, a backdoor encouragement that Peter would indeed attain *agape*. Yet Jesus also calls Peter to the only path of growing in love: a relentless and consistent following of Him.

If we are honest, most of us initially followed Jesus for self-centered reasons: hell avoidance, peace, forgiveness or a clean conscience, and unconditional love. Perhaps you wondered what the miracle-working God could do for you. Whatever our earlier motivations were, the only thing that will keep us following Him is love. When you love Jesus supremely, you will do *whatever* is required at the moment to follow Him, including loving others at great personal cost.

The first part of the love question is simply this: do you *agapeo* Jesus as He has loved you? If not, the only way to love this way is to follow Jesus more closely. We return to the love flywheel; we must see, experience, commit to, and do Christ's love again and again. As we receive His love, our love for Him increases and matures.

The second part of the love question is: do you *agapeo* others as He has loved you? With each response Peter gives to the question of loving Jesus, Jesus points him toward loving people. *Will you shepherd My sheep? Will you feed and care for others? Will you lead them to Me?* Again *agape* for others comes only after following Jesus.

There is no magic love pill that if taken twice daily will morph you into a more loving person. There is no self-improvement seminar that will give you three easy steps to sacrificial love. There is no phrase or mantra that, if repeated frequently enough, will meld your mind into love consciousness. Sacrificial love comes only as we experience Jesus' love and then follow Him radically in that love.

The Give and Take of Love

The nature of love is to give. Few will argue with this.[5] Many, however, will chafe at the idea that the point of love is to give without getting something back. Isn't that the love deal we broker in our relationships? We marry because we love our boyfriend (or girlfriend), but the fine print reads "so he/she will love me back." It's why many adults have children and even pets—they want someone or something to love them back.[6] A friend is someone who's got your back, not one who sticks knives in it. We can be quite generous and sacrificial in love so long as we're in a relationship that gives back. I'll scratch your itch, if you scratch mine.[7] It's the universal law of love, right?

Wrong.

Reciprocal love may be how the world understands love, but the believer is called to a higher standard. We are called to love based on who we've become as followers of Christ, not on what's in it for us. When clarifying love for other people, Jesus used the example of the good Samaritan. There is virtually nothing in His telling of this story that indicates that the Samaritan received any benefit or reciprocation. The Samaritan spent money and time and expended himself in caring for the needs of the half-dead man on the side of the road. He used his own first aid supplies and private transportation; he risked personal hygiene by getting dirty in cleaning wounds; he changed his travel agenda to meet the needs of someone incapable of giving back; he spent his hard-earned cash for room and board. Every act of love cost him something without reimbursement.

This does raise an important question: Can we love others and expect something in return? The short answer is no. When people love us, it should be welcomed, appreciated, and enjoyed. When we do loving actions to them with the motive or goal of having them love us back, we are acting selfishly. When love is expected, it is soon demanded and then coerced; humanly speaking, this is the inevitable and unfortunate direction human relationships take. Love ceases to be a free gift, but becomes a baited trap. If we love one another as Christ loved us, we do not love based on whether the other person loves us back or even appreciates our love.[8] We love because we've become loving people.

Love is its own reward. A friend, Ken, has a wife, Carol, who's survived a stroke with significant residual effects. She struggles with speech, creative thoughts, and basic motor skills. Her emotional and mental capacities are diminished; she must take powerful anti-seizure drugs. The intimacy they once shared is all but gone. What keeps him loving his wife is not her ability to love him back, but God's love being matured in him.

Greg Paul faced the undesirable task of cleaning up after a weak, dying AIDS patient had soiled himself.[9] Stop and think about that. What's the payoff for helping a grown man needing a sponge bath and a diaper change? What's the reward for loving someone who can't even love you back, even if they wanted? Joy. Really? Yes, joy. Joy is God's gift to the lover who gives to others without reward or recognition.

As a love hack in recovery, this part of love challenges me. When I wash the dishes, do laundry, or straighten the house, I want my wife to give me a medal and shower me with hugs. When I buy my college-aged sons clothes or top off the gas in their car, I'd like a little love coming back my direction. When I go into work early or stay late in order to give some second-mile service or provide some counseling to a couple, a pat on the back or bag of fresh coffee beans would be nice. Often when I love someone, I want to make sure that they know it, so that they, in turn, can tell me about my awesomeness. God is weaning me off my insatiable desire for love to boomerang each time I extend myself. Real love lives to give, not to get.

Once our demand for reciprocity of love is taken off the table, we're free to give sacrificially to those outside of our normal love perimeter. One of the biggest shockers for me in my studies on love is that *agape* is attributed to non-believers by none other than Jesus Himself.[10] I had been led to believe through years of church life that *agape* is something only Christians did. Jesus does refer to godless people having *agape*, but these people only love those who will love them back. Consequently, Jesus doesn't give this kind of love very high marks. His love doesn't demand a reimbursement. It's extended to all, not to a select few.[11] Jesus didn't demand reciprocity in His love, and neither should we.[12]

Most of us can't conceive of living a life of such radical love that extends itself to virtually everyone in our path. Mother Teresa is probably the best modern example we have of one whose love perimeter was so extended that it included all. Her tangible acts of love are legendary. She washed the dirty bodies of the abandoned low-caste men, women, and children of Calcutta. She fed those literally starving to death. She touched the untouchables and embraced orphaned infants. She gave dignity to all human life she encountered. What moved her to such a "profundity of pathos?"[13] Her first love was Jesus Christ—as the One who loved her deeply. Her second love was to Christ as He was seen in the least of these.[14]

Love clearly gives, but it also takes. Love takes risks—intentional acts that have no guaranteed results. Will love that's given be returned? Will it cost me more than I'm reimbursed? What if I'm hurt emotionally or taken advantage of financially? What if I give my all and the other person just gives twenty percent?

Love is not safe because it requires you to be genuinely exposed; you're left hanging "out there." If I'm so self-protective that I cannot be hurt, then I'm not in any position to love. "To love at all is to be vulnerable."[15] You simply can't love while being safe and stingy.

I am a risk taker; it's part of my wiring. Yet this creates an uncomfortable tension for me between putting my love out there for others and those who would potentially abuse that love. The tension is heightened by such passages in the Bible that tell us to go beyond the normal human response: take the second slap in the face, walk the second mile, give your stuff away, and refuse to press charges in a lawsuit.[16] When it comes to love, we're more likely to respond with the "eye for an eye" approach: I'll love you if (and only if) you'll love me. Otherwise, I'll pack up my toys and find someone else who will love fairly.

When I look at the life of Jesus, I don't see a man negotiating love deals that were reciprocal and risk-free. I see One who was threatened in one way or another throughout His public ministry—people from His hometown wanted to throw Him off a cliff, the religious leaders desired to kill Him quietly, even one of His own disciples betrayed Him (and even knowing this would happen, Jesus did not protect Himself from Judas). Jesus took a lot of abuse literally on the chin. His suffering and death was a living testimony of love absorbing evil, hatred, pain, and loss. He didn't enter into the defensive position of assault or withdrawal. He withstood all things done against Him while still loving God and others.

Will love cost me something? Will it hurt? Will it possibly be abused? Is it risky? Yes, yes, yes, and yes.

Choose love. Do it anyway.

When you contrast the strength of unlove and hate with that of love, you'll find that love is more powerful exactly because of its capacity to absorb all the negativity hurled at it and still stand strong. This power was released through the cross and resurrection of Jesus Christ; this same power is available to His followers today.

In order to sacrifice greatly, we must love deeply. Love gives a capacity to endure that gritted teeth and a resolute will alone cannot provide. One of the truest tests of love is not the heights to which it may soar, but the hells it will endure—even absorb—in giving itself away.

Perhaps you've heard of the counseling maxim that says, "Hurt people hurt people." The flip side of this is, "Loved people love people." When you have personally experienced the powerful and life-changing love of Jesus Christ, your deepest response to people should be to love them in the same way. This is how the world is changed. Loved people just love people. They absorb whatever hate and evil is flung at them and keep on loving people.

Jim Elliot was a missionary reaching the Acua Indians in Ecuador. He felt called to reach the Waodani people, a group known for their extreme hostility toward those outside of their tribe. After making initial contact with them through airplane flyovers, loud speakers, and parachuted gifts, Jim and four friends began to have personal contact with them. Then, surprisingly, they were tragically attacked and murdered by the Waodani. Later, in an act epitomizing *agape* love, his wife Elisabeth courageously continued to reach out to the very people who killed her husband. Through her kindness, forgiveness, and example of love, many came to faith in Christ. It was Christ's love in Jim and Elisabeth that enabled them to lovingly reach out to the Waodani people, even at incredible personal loss. Love absorbs evil and suffering, even to the death, and then rises to life and perseveres.

A Higher Love

Love of family and friends is widespread. You can find this kind of love in the city or countryside. It's found among the rich and poor, educated and uneducated, and across virtually all religious faiths and ethnic groups. Even the mafia and atheists enjoy the love of family and friends. The love that Jesus calls us to, however, is on a higher plane. Among His followers, this higher love separates the real deal from pretenders.

Three things should be noted when looking at the love Jesus taught and demonstrated and that which He expects of His followers.

Love is to be for all people.[17] The radical addition of Jesus to the world's understanding of love was its broad scope. Love wasn't just limited to family and friends—those who would inevitably love us back—but was offered to *all* people. All includes our enemies and those who can't or won't reciprocate our love. We are to love others not based on whether they deserve it or even desire it, but on love being deeply formed in our character as Christ-followers. The scope of Jesus' focus alone gives us a continual opportunity to grow in love.

Love is to be obvious to all people. Jesus promised that if we loved one another well, it would be obvious that we are His followers.[18] Jesus did not do love for the sake of calling attention to His individual acts of compassion, yet every act of love He did was humble, clear, and apparent. When Jesus loved people, there was no question if what He did was good and beneficial. Even as the Pharisees criticized His compassionate acts on the Sabbath, they didn't question the fact that what He did was gracious and kind. Simply said, love should be the defining and observable character trait of Christ-followers. If others can't plainly see our love, it's likely our fault, not theirs.

Love is to be Christlike. The crucial phrase of Jesus is "as I have loved you."[19] Jesus does not leave us to our own devices and definitions of love. He qualifies the love He commands. Simply, it is to be like His own. Through His teachings and examples and seen most clearly in His sacrificial death on the cross, we learn what love looks like. Consequently, we don't look to the world for our love cues—not pop psychology, romance novels, talk shows, or even marriage seminars. Our first and last word on love is Jesus Christ.

Make no mistake; such a love will rub against the grain of the world. There will be powerful and abusive social forces that will critique our love and seek to conform us to mediocrity and unlove. Some people will vehemently hate us regardless of how loving we may be. Love's ability to reach out vs. cave in can only be explained by the internal power of the Holy Spirit changing our lives and expanding our hearts to be more like Christ. A love that embodies these qualities will transform the world.[20]

CONFESSION OF A LOVE HACK
The Bad Samaritan

"We're on a mission for God!" This was our mantra and focus as four of us crammed our overstuffed luggage onto a commuter plane on the first leg of our journey. For everyone (except me) this was their first mission trip to Cambodia. Caffeine and adrenaline ran high. First stop: Chicago O'Hare. We were meeting the other half of our team in Seoul, Korea, and the margin of making our connecting flight was tight.

As team leader, I guided our group from the domestic concourse toward the international one. Knowing that we would need every spare minute to check in for the next flight, I pushed the pace. We snaked through the maze of walkways to the tram that connected terminals. When it seemed that we were far away from the regular crowds in the airport, we happened upon a scene.

A very bizarre scene, indeed.

A platinum blonde was lying face down on a heated floor vent. Did she trip? No. Our second impression was that she was a street person—disheveled blouse, no cosmetics, and a nearby luggage cart lent itself to this perspective. Perhaps she had a little too much to drink the night before. But there was more ... a little too much more.

Her pants were pulled down below her hips. Her backside was exposed for the entire world to see. We were all shocked speechless. I glanced away quickly. What was I supposed to do? I am a pastor and don't make it a habit of staring at semi-clad women. Worse yet, she was as still as a corpse ... grilling her face on the hot metal grate. One of the ladies on our team checked to see if she was still breathing. Her purse on the luggage cart was open. Perhaps she'd been robbed ... or raped? Where was airport security when you needed them?

Instead of listening to the (now) obvious voice of the Lord, I inclined my ear to the ticking clock. A connecting flight had to be made. Time was marching on … and so did we. In utter shame I realize in hindsight how much I was like the priest in the story of the good Samaritan, giving wide berth to a need that was so blatantly … exposed.

As team leader, my unlove was reprehensible. To this day our team is appalled at our unlove during that moment; we have all vowed to never let this happen again.

I saw Jesus naked and I did not clothe Him. Instead I hurried off on my "mission for God."

Lord, my unlove is not only inexcusable, but tragic. Forgive me for my heartless negligence of love and for leading others to do the same.

CHAPTER 9

The Love Test

"Whoever does not love abides in death."
1 John 3:14

"Biblical orthodoxy without compassion is
surely the ugliest thing in the world."
Francis A. Schaeffer

"At the end of life, we shall be judged by love."
St. John of the Cross

*F*ew places have the collective nervous energy of a college campus the week before and week of final exams. The stress is palatable; it lingers like the oppressive summer haze over Los Angeles. Some students channel that energy into marathon study sessions, combining intense concentration with copious amounts of caffeine resulting in a focused trance. Others buckle like a cheap lawn chair; they crater under the enormous load of information and understanding that needs to be downloaded in just a few days' time. Parties spontaneously erupt; zany behaviors emerge. Impeccable logic erodes into, "If I don't do well on the final, who cares? At least the semester will be over." *Que sera, sera.*

Test anxiety is nothing new. As long as there have been examinations, students have experienced sensations from mild butterflies to toxic bile in their stomachs. Tests are, after all, tests. They check on our progression toward mastery of a subject or skill. They reveal in a tangible way what we've learned ... or not. Nobody likes to be exposed for his or her ignorance in a subject. Tests can elate or humiliate; it all depends on your preparation and performance.

Not all tests are created equal either. In grad school I had one professor who designed his test to allow the student to show his or her breadth of knowledge in church music and worship. His final exam was twenty-four pages long and very comprehensive. The questions, however, were simple and straightforward, requiring only the capacity to regurgitate memorized data. In order to see how much the student knew, he even added a section at the end of the test: "Other things I have learned from this course." He wanted his students to succeed even if the test guaranteed a hand cramp.

Another theology professor preferred one question tests. My final exam was "Discuss the doctrine of God, including the Trinity, Scripture, and history in your answer." How do you handle that one?! Exactly how does one cover all of God, biblical revelation, and two thousand years of church history in a two-hour test? Tests like this cause us to think deeply, evaluate thoroughly, and distill succinctly the most important truths. No pat answers would suffice. You had to show that you had processed the information into a unified, holistic response.

The final judgment seat of Christ has, for good reason, been referred to as the ultimate final exam. This two-part test will include not only the pass–fail section, resulting in eternal life in heaven or eternal damnation in hell, but also the section evaluating the quality of one's character and works, resulting in heavenly rewards. It's *the* biggie. Understandably we have test anxiety about it.

We speculate all kinds of scenarios. *What if I'm asked a question I don't know the answer to? What if I'm miles off in my answers? What if it all goes down differently than what I've been taught in the* Left Behind *series?[1] Should I quote the KJV or NIV? Am I expected to know Greek and Hebrew? Will I be deducted points for poor spelling? Is there partial credit? Will I be graded on the curve?* Our questions about *the* questions ooze with anxiety.

What if all the issues boiled down to love?

Most of us would immediately breathe a huge sigh of relief. Ah, love … now that's a test we could pass. Then suddenly a seed of doubt germinates deep within our soul. This reservation gives us a creepy, visceral sensation that perhaps all is not right in our corner of the universe. *Would I pass the love test?* Gulp. Uh oh. *Do I love God supremely and others sacrificially?*

Que sera, sera, not so much.

The Eclipse of Love

In the ancient world, solar eclipses were often interpreted as menacing omens. Today, we see them as rare moments in our lifetimes to see something unusual. Solar eclipses are some of the more bizarre phenomena of nature. In predictable cycles, the orbit of the moon will cross in front of the sun. When this happens, daylight fades for a few moments and then returns as the exact alignment of the sun and moon passes. The sun hasn't disappeared, the moon just temporarily blocked its light. Love, as the central virtue of the Christian life, has been eclipsed for centuries. The resulting darkness looms ominously.

The starting point for the Reformation period is usually pinpointed to October 30, 1517 when Martin Luther nailed his *Ninety-Five Theses on the Power and Efficacy of Indulgences* on the door of the church in Wittenberg, Germany. He courageously stood up against the erroneous teachings of the Roman Catholic Church that then taught that a person might earn or buy his or her way into the good graces of God. Enough penance and cash guaranteed heaven. Luther renounced these abuses. He affirmed the simple, biblical understanding that people are made right with God through faith in Jesus Christ. Apart from a person's good works, salvation is offered to anyone who trusts in the perfect, complete, saving works of Jesus on his or her behalf. Luther staked his life on this teaching, and it resulted in a fresh move of God in Europe, into the New World, and fresh missionary zeal for new territories.

For the last five hundred years of evangelical church history, the watchword has been faith. If people would just believe, all would be well. Why, after all, are we called believers instead of lovers? Faith is the essential key to "being saved."[2] Faith has become the only acceptable answer to the evangelistic question: "If Jesus asked you why He should let you into heaven, what would you tell Him?" Faith in Jesus and right beliefs has reigned on the throne of biblical orthodoxy. I've personally bowed before this throne and encouraged others to do the same.

Now something deeper is nagging at my soul. I've become uneasy with the exaltation of faith at the expense of love. Love has been eclipsed out of the essential package of what it means to be a Christian. Why not have faith *and* love? Right beliefs should be 100 percent compatible with right living.

While I still affirm with a loud voice the importance of faith in Christ, I find the Bible pointing me back to the centrality of love. After all, the Great Commandment isn't *believe* God with all of your heart, soul, mind, and strength, but *love* Him. Comprehension of biblical knowledge and having a faith that can move mountains is *nothing* without love. In the scales, love carries more weight than faith; of the three virtues that remain—faith, hope, and love—love is the greatest. The parable of the sheep and goats in Matthew 25 tells us that it's tangible love that is the final criterion for heaven. Faith may open the door, but love is what makes us fit for heaven.[3]

Jesus tells us that we will express our love for Him through obedience to His commandments. The red-letter commandments of Jesus often focus on loving God and others, not getting all the answers right on a theological quiz. Faith in Jesus, apart from a loving relationship with Him, rings hollow. Love recalibrates faith to be about the person of Jesus, not detached orthodox confessions about Him.

Unfortunately our churches today have valued orthodoxy, excellence, and the need to be right over love, grace, and relationships. This issue is a touchy razor's edge. I'm certainly in favor of clear, biblical thinking and excellence in ministry, but I'm also strongly convinced that without love, what we call theological orthodoxy isn't even orthodox. Ask yourself two probing questions: *In my life, am I more obsessed with being right or with loving? Am I driven more by excellent performance or my love being qualitatively like Christ?* These same questions apply to the church.

We like the black and white of issues so that we can know we're believing and doing the right things. The clarity of truth helps us have God's perspective, right? We keep trying to eat from the tree of the knowledge of good and evil, but in so doing, we miss the tree of life. Love is the fruit that gives life without pride or shame. As we focus on *love* rejoicing with the truth—not truth per se—we'll find the balance that we so desperately need today.

It's time to remove all hindrances, theological or otherwise, that block out the bright light of love. The eclipse of love has lasted long enough.

Love in the Last Days

I'm always amazed at the audacity of people who write volumes and draw elaborate timelines related to the return of Christ. Although Jesus Himself said that He didn't know the day or hour of His return, these geniuses are undeterred. The Lord may be clueless, but they know the month and year. They know exactly how history will unfold. They've figured out the mysteries of eternity and mapped them out chronologically on color-coded charts. Call me a skeptic, but I am just not convinced. What's more, I'm less interested in ordering the events in the future and more concerned about following Christ in the present day.

How should we live today that honors Christ, expresses love to Him and others, and prepares us (and others) for our eternal destiny? Jesus' focus on His second return wasn't so much about all the ordering of events as ordering our lives to be ready for His sudden return. Tucked away in His lengthy explanations of end times in Matthew 24–25 is this short, powerful indictment of unlove:

> And then many will fall away and betray one another and *hate one another.* And many false prophets will arise and lead many astray. And because lawlessness will be increased, *the love of many will grow cold.* But the one who endures to the end will be saved. And this gospel of the kingdom will be proclaimed throughout the whole world as a testimony to all nations, and then the end will come. (Matt. 24:11–14; emphasis mine)

During the end times chaos, love is rare while unlove is common. The short phrase, *the love of many will grow cold,* should arouse us out of our relational slumber. *Our* love can slide from white-hot to icy cold. There's no indication here that it will happen suddenly or obviously, as if you quickly turn off the hot faucet and immediately turn on the cold one. The slippery slope of unlove has a gentle grade. The transition will be so gradual and negligible that it will be hardly noticed by anyone … except God. Cold, lifeless love is the charge levied against *many*, not just a few on the fringe. How do masses of believers in Jesus fade on one of His central teachings? As lawlessness increases, love decreases. Low morals and high peer pressure are the breeding grounds for unlove.

In the summers, my wife can sleep comfortably under blankets while the boys and I hardly even use sheets. In the winter, she can't get warm enough through hot coffee, electric blankets, and scalding showers. It's easy for me to tell when she's cold by her body language. Her shoulders pull forward and in, she crosses her arms in an X over her chest, and becomes immobile in an effort to conserve her own body heat. When our love grows cold, it's evidenced by our body language. We pull in to ourselves. Life is no longer about giving ourselves away in love but protecting ourselves from loss. The overall social pressure to conform to the world ruthlessly pounds on our souls until we relent and just stop loving. Little by little our love erodes into unlove.

In the stressful times of World War II, love was one of many casualties. During the Holocaust, many church-going people were faced with the dilemma of helping the Jews or focusing on self-preservation. Sadly, the percent of lovers was quite low. The same unfortunate truth repeats itself virtually every generation: one need only to reflect on the tragedies in Cambodia, Bosnia, Rwanda, human trafficking, and wherever genocide, war, terrorism, and organized crime thrive. When our very existence is put on the line, our love is given a defining temperature check. Although Laurie and I have never been directly in a situation akin to the Holocaust, we have speculated about what we would do. Honestly, I fear my love for others is way too chilly. I don't want to die as a completely useless love hack.

Jesus says that only the ones who endure to the end will be saved. Endure what? The ability to sustain love fits the context best. Endurance isn't measured by how deeply you embed your fingernails in the wall of heaven and hold on for dear life. It's measured by how you keep on loving God and others while the rest of the world self-destructs. "Love bears all things, believes all things, hopes all things, endures all things. Love never ends."4 Only a love rooted in the life of God will last to the end. All others will cool and die. The final exam may be love-based after all.5

The parable of the sheep and the goats is the final words of Jesus on his discussion of end times. Even if you're familiar with it, it's worth reading again.

> When the Son of Man comes in his glory, and all the angels with him, then he will sit on his glorious throne. Before him will be gathered all the nations, and he will separate people one from another as a shepherd separates the sheep from the goats. And he will place the sheep on his right, but the goats on the left. Then the King will say to those on his right, "Come, you who are blessed by my Father, inherit the kingdom prepared for you from the foundation of the world. For I was hungry and you gave me food, I was thirsty and you gave me drink, I was a stranger and you welcomed me, I was naked and you clothed me, I was sick and you visited me, I was in prison and you came to me." Then the righteous will answer him, saying, "Lord, when did we see you hungry and feed you, or thirsty and give you drink? And when did we see you a stranger and welcome you, or naked and clothe you? And when did we see you sick or in prison and visit you?' And the King will answer them, 'Truly, I say to you, as you did it to one of the least of these my brothers, you did it to me."
>
> Then he will say to those on his left, "Depart from me, you cursed, into the eternal fire prepared for the devil and his angels. For I was hungry and you gave me no food, I was thirsty and you gave me no drink, I was a stranger and you did not welcome me, naked and you did not clothe me, sick and in prison and you did not visit me." Then they also will answer, saying, "Lord, when did we see you hungry or thirsty or a stranger or naked or sick or in prison, and did not minister to you?" Then he will answer them, saying, "Truly, I say to you, as you did not do it to one of the least of these, you did not do

it to me." And these will go away into eternal punishment, but the righteous into eternal life. (Matt. 25:31–46)

The criterion for the final judgment is love expressed tangibly to "the least of these." The sheep do love, the goats don't. Sheep love even the people on the farthest margins of life, the ones that Christ Himself has identified with. The goats never made it past their family and friends. Goats have a fantastic excuse for their unlove: We just didn't know it was You, Lord. Ultimately, it's their *negligence of love*, not their ignorance of Jesus, that seals their fate. In the big scheme of things, the cost of loving now far outweighs the cost of unlove eternally. Love and unlove is a high-stakes game with life-altering consequences.[6]

While this parable clearly teaches some powerful and shocking truths about the final judgment, it also tells us about how we are to love all people today. Each of us is individually called to love beyond our normal relationship circles, to step out and do love to the least of these. Mother Teresa says,

> Being happy with Him [Jesus] now means loving like He loves, helping like He helps, giving as He gives, serving as He serves, rescuing as He rescues, being with Him twenty-four hours a day, touching Him in His distressing disguise.[7]

If we say that we love Jesus whole-heartedly, we must also realize that His "distressing disguise" looks exactly like the very people we're least likely to serve. We'd rather ignore the hungry, glance away from the naked, neglect the sick, and forget about the imprisoned. We justify our behavior by saying that it was their own poor decisions that put them in the fix they're in. AIDS? That what happens when you engage in risky, immoral behavior. Food stamps? Should have gotten a better job. Diabetes? Should have passed on those Krispy Kremes. And just like that we've taken the left side of the throne with the other unloving, self-justifying goats.[8]

Unlove isn't even considered an option when you're an oblivious sheep. Sheep may be blissfully ignorant of whom they love, but Christ's life of love has been so deeply woven into their lives that they just do it anyway. Their love isn't flashy or even extraordinary, just real. The test of our profession of love for the invisible God without any needs is how we love the visible people around us with real needs. [9]

The Answer is Love

Algebra's one of those subjects in school that you might be able to work out the correct answer in your head, but the teacher will still count off points for your failure to show your work. She's more interested in how you arrived at your answer—the methodology—than in the rightness of your response. The steps used to get the right answer must be shown in the hopes that you can prove that you didn't just pull the answer out of thin air ... or off of your neighbor's homework.

What if you were given the final exam on the first day of the semester? What if you were even given the correct answer? What if all that was required was for you to show your work? Could you?

What if you were told on the day that you believed in Jesus that the final judgment would be based on the development of God's love in your life? You are given the final question and answer; could you show your work?

The love test isn't a series of trick questions designed to trip you up. It's actually not very complicated. It's simply a test God gives to us early on in our walk with Him. From our first moments of faith in Jesus to our standing before Him at the Great White Throne, love is central to all He's asking of us: *Do you love Me with all you are and do you love all the different kinds of people around you?* He's clued us in to the question and even the answer. Now He wants you and me to show our work. *Now* is the time to do love.

CONFESSION OF A LOVE HACK

A Repulsive Heart

It was an assault on my senses.

I wandered through the maze of stalls in the open-air Phsar Thmei market in Phnom Penh. I was there just to grab a handful of souvenirs for my family after a week of teaching rural Cambodian pastors. My outbound flight to the United States was just hours away. Time was ticking.

The pungent smells of ripe fruit and the unrefrigerated butchery mixed in the air with smoldering trash and burning incense. Colorful silk fabrics lined the narrow aisles with oranges, yellows, and reds. The hum and hammer of sewing machines whirled in the hidden recesses of the plastic-tarp walls. Aggressive Cambodian hawkers battered my ears with "I give you good price! Please look!" while pulling at my arms and holding up some unique trinket. Sweat trickled down my back as I clenched my backpack tightly to prevent pickpockets and petty thieves from taking advantage of another "rich Westerner."

In my rush to see all the shopping options, I became separated from my team. Within minutes, I rounded a blind corner of a remote area of the market and came face-to-face with a beggar. By face-to-face, I mean literally face-to-face. We could breathe on each other we were so close.

I recoiled, visibly shocked by the disfigurement of his face. It was as if someone poured a gallon of hot wax under his skin on one side of his head. It was puffy and hung like the loose jowls of a bulldog. Cambodia's tragic history of war and poverty converged on this one face—probably a birth-defect from exposure to toxic chemicals used in the Vietnam War.

I quickly turned away and headed down another aisle. My pulse pounded and for several seconds my only thought was to run. Fast. Get away from what freaked me out.

As my breathing returned to normal and as I regrouped my senses, I was disgusted. Not at the hideous face, but at my own monstrous reaction. I had just flinched noticeably at a person's appearance. A handicapped beggar who has lived a life of rejection just got another dose from yours truly.

I saw the "least of these" face-to-face and bolted. No grace, no gift, no help, no love. All I did was distance myself from a real person in need. My heart was far more repulsive than this man's face could ever be.

Lord, save others from my lovelessness. May my visceral reaction be love and acceptance to You in your "distressing disguise."

CHAPTER 10

The Love People

"May the Lord make you increase and abound
in love for one another and for all."
1 Thessalonians 3:12

"Love of enemies is perhaps Jesus' teaching that
is most famous and most violated."
John Ortberg

"What we think or what we believe is, in the end, of little consequence.
The only thing of consequence is what we do."
John Ruskin

The Westboro Baptist Church of Topeka, Kansas, hates fags. For them, this identifies them as God's people. Their website, www. godhatesfags.com, spews their scorn for homosexuality and America in general. Their claim to fame is picketing the funerals of soldiers and law enforcement officers with signs and placards declaring that God caused these deaths as a punishment for our country's lack of morality. By cleverly hiding behind their First Amendment rights for the freedom of religious expression, they've protected themselves from legal action. Public sentiment finds their actions socially distasteful at best and an incarnation of evil at worst. They are not merely advocating for hate; they are fully committed to it.[1]

On June 28, 2010, a portion of the Westboro congregation showed up in my current town of Owasso, Oklahoma. While the rest of our city honored the sacrifice of army Sgt. Andrew Looney, a small contingent of

Westboro members, including two of their children, protested with hate signs and slogans. The outrageous nature of their actions received wholesale condemnation for using our town as their platform for animosity. Grief mixed with some hostility at their lovelessness was expressed.

What kinds of people call themselves Christians and drag God into their ranting hate? Sadly, unlove is even institutionalized in some churches.[2] The Westboro folks are not known as the love people. They flaunt their hate with as much intensity, if not more, than the gay-lesbian-transgender community parades its sexuality publicly. There are no winners when the contest is between hate pride and gay pride.

Before you and I get out our poster board and markers and create our own "God Hates Westboro Idiots!" signs, we need to pause and reflect on an important question. If we were completely honest, what would *our* signs read? Who might be the group(s) of people that we would prefer to exclude from our love circle? Terrorists? Muslims? Communists? Democrats or Republicans? Greedy capitalists? Abortionists? Politicians? People on welfare? Insurance CEOs? The DMV desk clerk? The list is endless with nationalities, races, tribes, religions, genders, and personal preferences and dislikes. If our signs were truthful, we'd all see the deep-seated biases we have toward certain groups of people. Though our signs are unwritten, they are read by all through our actions, however subtle or blatant. Christians as a whole, not just the Westboro church, are unfortunately not known as the love people.

This unfortunate reality must change. It's time for love to become more than a sweet nicety that we add to our list of Christian virtues. Love must dominate all aspects of our lives so that we are known as the love people.

It's time to rewrite our signs to reflect the heart of Jesus. God loves *everyone*, including you and me. No one is excluded.[3] His nature *is* love, and He acts loving to both the wicked and the righteous. Once our signs are corrected, it's time to live according to that new reality. This doesn't mean that you have no convictions about important moral or social issues, but it does mean that you'll have a stronger conviction to love people than to judge them.

Word Association

When Laurie and I were dating, we used to play a dangerous verbal game—word association. In rapid-fire succession, one of us would rattle off a series of words and the other person would respond as quickly as possible with whatever word popped up in their thoughts. I say this was a dangerous game precisely because it was so fast-paced that any mental filter we might have had in place was eventually overloaded. Ultimately, our real self would jump out of our mouths. The words were usually quite common: salt, light, stick, dog, water, hill, etc. Our answers were often unpredictable.

We discovered a tendency that still plagues our marriage to this day. She thinks in synonyms while I think in antonyms. She says *dog*, I say *cat*. But if I say *dog*, she says *Fritz* (the name of her childhood dog). She says *hill*, I say *valley*. I say *hill*, she says *mountain*. You get the picture. Our tendencies to this oppositional way of thinking have led to some hilarious, and at times frustrating, misfires over the years. Word association reveals our connections and disconnections with each other's thinking and perceptions.

Chances are if you are still reading the last chapter in this book, you are a Christ-follower. May I challenge you with an equally dangerous game? Play word association with some people who do not believe in Jesus. Start them off with some easy stuff—nature, work, cars, pets, colors, whatever. At random points, throw in words like Christian, evangelical, born-again, church, Bible-believer, and follower of Jesus. What I can virtually guarantee is that you won't hear the word love in association with any of these words related to following Jesus. What you will likely hear are words related to being judgmental, narrow-minded, stupid/ignorant, homophobic, rightwing, or even hate-filled. How is it that the one group of people in the whole world who should be known for love is not identified as such? To borrow a phrase from James, "My brothers, these things ought not to be so!"[4] This may be the greatest avoidable tragedy of the twenty-first century.

Of all the traits that Jesus said should identify His followers, He singled out love. Shouldn't we be concerned that we are not known as the love people? Shouldn't we be grieved that we're more known for what we are *against* than what we are *for*? If our love is so diminished that unbelievers have a hard time seeing it, should we even be identified as *Christ*-followers, since He said that His followers would love God and others?

The current perception among unbelievers is that Christians don't love; this *is* their reality. Whether or not their perception is correct can be debated elsewhere. More often than not, perception has at least one leg standing in reality. Their understanding of Christians being hypocrites is deeply ingrained in their minds and has some legitimacy to it.

Hypocrisy is the one word that sums up their view that the walk and talk of Christians is incongruent. The Lord of love that believers profess isn't anything like the life they live every day. As a result, Christianity is often the legitimate target of a scathing critique from the media and society as a whole. The logic is quite simple and succinct:

A: Christians are supposed to love God and people.

B: Christians don't.

Ergo: Christians are hypocrites.

It's pretty hard to argue that *A* isn't true. The clear command of Christ and the teaching of the Bible are that we are to love God and others. Is the assessment of *B* really accurate? Certainly there is room for interpretation or perception to be distorted from personal experience. Perhaps *B* should read, "Christians don't love perfectly … or obviously … or consistently." Yet the fact remains and is hard to dismiss that the general consensus of unbelievers is that Christians don't love well.

Until the unbelievers are more convinced of our love, we should face the delusion that our love isn't as vibrant and healthy as we would think. We're better in our minds than in reality. Our intentions may be inspired by Christ but our lifestyles are disconnected from Him. We, as a group and as individuals, are love hacks. With the current state of the church, the *ergo* of unbelievers seems justified.[5] The world understands that a loveless Christian is a contradiction of terms. Do we? The one thing that should clearly characterize our lives as followers of Christ—love— has been found lacking and its absence has become the very thing that condemns us.

This judgment hurts; it's agonizing. It hurts emotionally to know that our love hasn't been so obvious or perhaps the realization of how weak it is. It hurts intellectually to know there are some painful truths we need to hear. It hurts spiritually to know that our love for Christ and people is so negligible that it doesn't make a ripple on the water for the kingdom. Until we see our unlove as a serious spiritual crisis—the equivalent of denying that Jesus is the Son of God—we will not be sufficiently moved to the radical loving actions we must take to change ourselves and then the world around us. In the scales, our unlove speaks louder than our evangelism.

It's time for a lovequake. It's time for God's love to powerfully shake the foundations of the church. It's time to return our faith in Christ to a simple, loved-based lifestyle where God is loved supremely and people are loved tangibly. It's time for love to flow through each Christ-follower to those around him with the life-changing grace and love of Jesus Christ. It's time to reclaim love as the central, dominant, and life-giving way of Jesus Christ.[6] It's time to love God and people so radically that the media is confounded through the irrefutable evidence of love. It's time to shake off our hypocrisy and establish the credibility of Christian love. A love revolution is needed.

Back in the Day

We all have our own "back in the day" stories. Perhaps it was the proverbial walk to school … ten miles … uphill both ways … in the snow … with the wind in your face and sun in your eyes. We love to talk about when gas was cheaper and when hardships were worse. The fish were bigger, our sporting prowess greater, and food tastier—back in the day. My sons roll their eyes whenever I bring up a back-in-the-day story, such as having to ride my bike several miles to junior high in all kinds of weather conditions while carrying books, a tennis racket, and a baritone. Now that they are entering college, they are starting to voice their own versions of back in the day. Apparently, the back-in-the-day syndrome is contagious.

As hard as it may be to imagine today, a time existed when love so characterized the lives of believers that their love was undeniable. During the first three centuries after Christ's resurrection—back in the day—love dominated their community life. As early as AD 124, Aristides defended the Christian faith to the Roman emperor Hadrian. At risk of his own life, Aristides confessed this about Christians:

> They do good to their enemies; and their women, O King, are pure as virgins, and their daughters are modest; and their men keep themselves from every unlawful union and from all uncleanness, in the hope of a recompense to come in the other world. Further, if one or other of them have bondmen and bondwomen or children, through love towards them they persuade them to become Christians, and when they have done so, they call them brethren without distinction. They do not worship strange gods, and they go their way in all modesty and cheerfulness. Falsehood is not found among them; and they love one another, and from widows they do not turn away their esteem; and they deliver the orphan from him who treats him harshly. And he, who has, gives to him who has not, without boasting. And when they see a stranger, they take him in to their homes and rejoice over him as a very brother; for they do not call them brethren after the flesh, but brethren after the spirit and in God. And whenever one of their poor passes from the world, each one of them according to his ability gives heed to him and carefully sees to his burial. And if they hear that one of their number is imprisoned or afflicted on account of the name of their Messiah, all of them anxiously minister to his necessity, and if it is possible to redeem him they set him free. And if there is among them any that is poor and needy, and if they have no spare food, they fast two or three days in order to supply to the needy their lack of food.[7]

Could such a defense be made today of your life or mine? If placed before a jury, would the evidence from our lives exonerate our love or condemn our unlove?

Often it was the Christians who regularly went through the cities to pick up abandoned children, care for those left to die with plague, or give shelter and food to neglected widows. Clement (AD 150–215) described a man who "impoverished himself out of love, so that he is certain he may never overlook a brother in need." Justin Martyr's defense of the Christian faith (AD 155) included a love and unity that replaced hate and division. In AD 200, Tertullian reported that the Roman unbelievers would exclaim, "See how they love one another!"[8] The early church's defense was love, not defensiveness about their love. They could point to tangible acts of love and say, "What do you say to that!?" The obvious goodness of their love ultimately silenced their critics.

When was the last time you heard an atheist confess amazement at how much love the Christians in your town (or church) have for each other? Even once in your lifetime? I've heard many churches smugly defend their love; but few to zero unbelievers are convinced. This is true of even *my* church; what about yours? In communities across America, love isn't one of the top words out of mouth of unbelievers when describing Christians.

The kingdom of God spread in the early centuries of the Christian era due to people following the simple command of Jesus to love. The growth of the ancient church wasn't due to a compelling vision statement or an elaborate strategy or organizational flowchart. Growth happened because the love of Jesus was irresistible when tangibly demonstrated through His followers. In essence, love *was* the vision. Love *was* the strategy. Back in the day, the Christians were undeniably the love people.

What about Today?

If unbelievers have difficulty seeing our love, and if in the past Christ-followers did have a clear and compelling lifestyle of love, then we need to shoulder the reality that today we've drifted off course. Our love has shifted; it's been downgraded from the "greatest of these" virtue to a secondary or even optional way of life. Christlike love today is more of our backup plan when all of our own relational machinations implode or fail. Integrity demands that we openly confess that we're love hacks and not the love people of Jesus.

How did Christian love fizzle out over time? Simply put, believers became distracted. Their values shifted away from love to secondary things. At various places along the historical timeline, the criteria for what makes one spiritual evolved while love has consistently been pushed into the background. In the Middle Ages, monasticism was the pinnacle of Christian spirituality. During the Reformation, orthodox theology reigned as king. Pietism focused on personal spiritual growth through prayer. Revivalists and missionaries have focused on conversions. Charismatics say that speaking in tongues or demonstrating the more dramatic gifts constitute spiritual vitality. Mainline churches focus on faithfulness to God with a nonjudgmental attitude. The catch phrase today among postmoderns is social justice. While most of these things have a clear value in living out our faith, when they are devoid of love, it's disastrous. The demotion of love, however unintentionally, means that love no longer is seen as the most important way to demonstrate our obedience to Jesus Christ.

One doesn't have to look far to find a church full of relationship carnage and the effects of unlove. Church splits, hostile leadership meetings, toxic gossip, smug cliques, arrogant showmanship on the platform, complaints about ministries, grumbling about leaders, and the general neglect of reaching out to those in need of Christ or help in general—these are just a few of the symptoms of unlove that have infected our churches. Unfortunately, there are also countless thousands who simply quit going to church and avoid "institutional religion" because of some unloving words said or heartless act done to them decades ago. The cost of loving people is great, but the cost of not loving them is even higher. The stakes simply don't get higher than eternity.

Change is needed. Now.

We can't wait for the next generation to get it right. *We* need to be the incarnation of Christ's love today.

Christine Caine, a fiery Greek who grew up in Australia, co-pastors Hillsong Church. She founded the A21 Campaign, a ministry that fights injustice and human trafficking. Once while she was comforting a recently rescued Russian sex slave, Christine explained to her about the God who loves her. The young lady asked a bold, penetrating question, "If what you say about God is true, why didn't you come sooner?"[9]

If our God is the God of love, then why aren't we loving like He is? Unlove is not an option. Love is the urgent need for the world today. Today—as in now.

Heart Monitor

Endurance athletes often monitor all kinds of stats for their bodies: hydration, calories burned, pulse rate, pace, and so on. By studying this feedback and making minor adjustments, they are able to tweak their performances to achieve maximum output. For a handful of dollars, you can buy a personal heart monitor that electronically measures and records your heart rate. You can know if you are reaching your desired pulse rate during exercise or while eating potato chips and watching TV.

Solomon once said, "Keep your heart with all vigilance, for from it flow the springs of life."[10] The heart is the executive control center of our lives. So goes the heart, so goes the person. If we fall asleep while guarding our hearts, our love drifts. Unlove settles in. Our hearts need a monitor to notify us when our love levels dip dangerously low.

The Spirit of Jesus is that heart monitor. He lives inside of every believer. He speaks encouragement and truth. He empowers and enables. He creates and forms the love of Jesus within each heart. Sometimes He whispers, other times He yells. But His goal of making us to be love people is never thwarted or diminished. The fruit of the Spirit is love, and this is how we know Him.

One of the most beautiful letters in the New Testament was written to the church at Ephesus. In the first three chapters, Paul waxes eloquently about the grace and love of God in Christ Jesus. In the last three chapters, Paul demonstrates what love looks like in daily relationships with other believers, family members, and coworkers. The relative brevity of this book combined with the high quality of Greek grammar and vocabulary make many scholars think that Ephesians is the pinnacle of Paul's writing career.

So what happened to the Ephesian Christians? Their love shifted. Their hearts grew cold. They weren't diligent in their vigilance. How do we know this?

Another letter was written to the Ephesians—not by Paul, but by John. In Revelation 2, Jesus says:

> I know your works, your toil, and your patient endurance, and how you cannot bear with those who are evil, but have tested those who call themselves apostles and are not, and found them to be false. I know you are enduring patiently and bearing up for my name's sake, and you have not grown weary. *But I have this against you, that you have abandoned the love you had at first.* Remember therefore from where you have fallen; *repent, and do the works you did at first.* If not, I will come to you and remove your lampstand from its place, unless you repent. (Rev. 2:2-5; emphasis added)

The Ephesians receive a stinging rebuke: they abandoned love.[11] The Greek word for *abandon* means to leave behind or to divorce. Their once vibrant love cooled into unlove. They divorced themselves from love. Their love fire had burned down, and now it was time to rekindle it. Jesus Himself threatened to remove their lampstand. If they did not change their hearts soon, their very existence as a church was in jeopardy. The churches of Christ in America stand at such a crossroad. Like the Ephesians, we are called to repent and take action.

Repent. Repent is one of those words that make it sound as though we need to beat ourselves up spiritually in order to let God know we're serious about sin. Actually, it simply means we need to change. If you miss the turn you're supposed to take, the annoying voice of your GPS will notify you that you need to turn around. If you ignore the voice, you'll just continue driving in the wrong direction or waste precious time in finding a new route. Repent means you turn around and take the correct turn that God has indicated. If you don't change course, you will end up exactly where you are heading … in the wrong direction.

One of the ways we repent is by *admitting openly to God and others that we are love hacks.* None of us loves flawlessly. We simply need to tell God that we are sorry that we are not living the life of love that He's called us to (Eph. 5:2). We have not followed Jesus in love. We've not heeded the voice of the Holy Spirit. We also need to tell those around us that we have not loved them well. Often times, a humble admission of this to someone we are trying to love will be the first real act of love to them. I can't count the times I've had to acknowledge to my wife and children that I am a love hack and am genuinely sorry for the consequences that this brings in their lives.

We need to *get real about our love motivations*. Most of us have a system of "invest and return" built into our psyche. If we invest effort, time, and action into a relationship, we expect a payoff in the end. The returns on our love investments may be material blessings, Brownie points with God, personal happiness, influence over others, or just being liked. None of these things are promised by God. When we love based on these motivations, we inevitably love with conditions attached. *Agape* eludes us. God loves because He *is* love, and love is its own reward. Until love is deeply formed in our nature through the work of the Spirit, we need to repent of these self-centered motivations.

We also need to *change our standards for spiritual maturity*. More often than not, we attempt to quantify spiritual maturity in terms of spiritual disciplines (such as Bible study, prayer, stewardship) or ministry "numbers" (baptisms, church attendance, people involved in a ministry).[12] When Christlike love becomes the criterion for spiritual maturity, we will find all other standards appalling.

Brennan Manning tells of a time when he was asked to share a word with a Christian organization known for their discipleship programs. He simply asked a question: "Instead of being identified as a community that memorizes Scripture, why not be identified as a community of professional lovers that causes people to say, 'How they love one another!'?"[13] Love alone is the evidence that we have passed out of death into life.[14] Repentance is needed *anytime* love is diminished.

Do Love. It's not enough to admit the need for change without actually changing. As we do new things, it demonstrates change. Because love is action-oriented, when the actions cease, love is lost or forsaken. Love is recovered through actions. We are to be a living incarnation of Jesus' love to the people around us. The love and life of Jesus is to flow through *your body* to others around you.

So what are you to actually do? Start with the "one-anothers" outlined in chapter 7 (love is kind, humble, serving, caring, welcoming; it speaks the truth and values relationship). The key to doing love is uncomplicated obedience to Jesus. Focus on doing loving actions that are simple and clear. When things start getting too complicated or appear optional, it's time to back up and refocus on simple acts of love.

In many sports, coaches teach the economy of motion. This means that only bodily activities that work toward the ultimate goal are pursued. This is why Tour de France cyclists have huge thighs but relatively small pecs. This is why swimmers streamline their strokes, why runners find their stride, why gymnasts work on grip strength. No actions are wasted. Movements that are effective and powerful are repeated *ad infinitum*.

When we love, we don't need to waste our actions on things that are self-centered, ineffective, or fuzzy. Simple love is most effective because it just obeys Jesus without wasting efforts on secondary things. We love with no manipulations, no hype, and no showboating: simple love based on uncomplicated obedience to Jesus.

Who are we to love? Everyone! To borrow a phrase from singer Stephen Stills and reinterpreting it in light of Jesus, "love the one you're with." Are you a stay-at-home mom surrounded with preschoolers? Love them. Are you employed by some large corporation and quarantined in a high-rise full of cubicles? Love the people around you. Are you in a lunchroom and notice someone being marginalized? Love him or her. Are you sitting next to your friends (or complete strangers) in a church service? Love them. What about that clerk at the convenience store or the waitress at the diner or the overly zealous parent yelling at the Little League baseball game? What about that elderly widow down the street or the homeless man pushing the grocery cart of his worldly goods or the maintenance man who's been ignored as just a piece of landscape in the forest of humanity?

Love requires a unique set of skills—the ability to keep one eye scanning the horizon for people around you and one ear listening carefully to the Spirit's promptings. We are with far more people than we acknowledge. People are everywhere, so love the ones you're with.[15]

Two things are certain: Love requires action and relationships. If we avoid either of these two essential ingredients, we simply won't love. When we do real acts of love with real people around us, it reverses the slippery slide into unlove. Love is the antidote to unlove.

Be Love

Bruce Lee's skill as a pure martial artist has been surpassed by few. He was the consummate fighter's fighter. In an interview related to the philosophy of martial arts, he said: "Water can flow or it can crash. Be water, my friend." Elsewhere he said, "Be like water making its way through cracks. Do not be assertive, but adjust to the object, and you shall find your way around or through it." Water is fluid and can adapt its shape around whatever is placed in it. In this sense, it is soft. Water is powerful when unleashed forcefully as in a flashflood or tidal wave. In this sense, water is hard. To *be* water means to *act* like water—that is, to share the properties of water.

We are to *be* love so that we *act* like love. Whatever the properties of love are, we are to internalize them to the degree that our external lives look and act like love. What are these essential properties?

- Love should be like Jesus' love. Incarnational. Sacrificial. Unconditional.
- Love should be seen in actions. Love is only expressed through tangible actions. Invisible love benefits no one.
- Love is for the good of others. Regardless if they deserve it or whether they reciprocate, love is extended for the good of others.

God's love has been lavished on us through Jesus. As we receive and experience His love, God makes us more loving. It's our new nature in Him to love. We're not just trying to conjure up love, but God loves the world through us. "God loved the world so much that He gave Jesus. Today He loves the world so much that He gives you and me to be His love, His compassion, and His presence."[16]

"Christ has no body on earth but yours,
no hands but yours,
no feet but yours.
Yours are the eyes through which Christ's
compassion for the world is to look out;
yours are the feet with which He is to go about doing good;
and yours are the hands with which He is to bless us now."
St. Teresa of Avila

Be love. Do love. Repeat.

ENDNOTES

Chapter 1: Love Hack

1. Incarnational love will be covered in more depth in later chapters, especially chapter 4. It refers to actions that are expressed through a human body.
2. 1 John 3:14.
3. 1 Corinthians 13:2–3.
4. John 13:34.
5. Luke 9:51–56.
6. Mark 10:35–41.
7. 1 John 4:7–21.
8. 1 Timothy 1:12–17.
9. John 5:19.
10. 1 John 3:16; 4:10–11.

Chapter 2: Love Sick

1. Gary Chapman, *The Five Love Languages: The Secret to Love that Lasts*, (Chicago: Northfield Publishing, 2010), 19.
2. 1 John 4:7, 16.
3. Simon May, *Love: A History* (New Haven: Yale University Press, 2011), 14, says, "If love in the Western world has a founding text, that text is Hebrew. Before Plato and Aristotle . . . and well before Jesus, Hebrew Scriptures provides, in two pithy sentences, ideas that have guided the course of love ever since: 'You shall love the Lord your God with all your heart, and with all your soul, and with all your might' and 'You shall love your neighbour [sic] as yourself.'"
4. Matthew 22:40
5. Luke 10:28
6. Dallas Willard, "Getting Love Right: A Paper Presented at the American Association of Christian Counselors Conference" (September 15, 2007), Kindle Edition, says that the New Testament writers make *agape* love "the indispensable centrality."

7.   1 Corinthians 13:1–3.

8.   1 Corinthians 13:13

9.   Colossians 3:12–14; 2 Peter 1:5–7.

10. 1 John 2:9–11; 3:14–18, 23–24; 4:7–5:2.

11. In an effort to keep this definition short, I have omitted the assumed qualifiers that God is the author of all love, and good is defined by God.

12. My observation is that most people fall into the "deep or wide" camps. The "deep" camp loves those closest to them with great commitment, but has virtually no love for those outside their narrowly-defined relationship world. Those in the "wide" camp try to love everyone, but often with a soft and superficial love that is more akin to a bumper sticker slogan than actual actions that benefit others. Jesus' love was both deep and wide. He loved all and He loved them deeply.

13. Love is the backdrop for all of the "hard" sayings of Jesus, such as the call to take up the cross, die to self, or sell all of one's possessions. If God is loved supremely and completely, and if we love other people sacrificially, these "hard sayings" will seem easy by comparison. According to John 14:15, love precedes obedience. Therefore, we don't obey our way into love; we love our way into obedience. With this in mind, this is why love is the root of the Great Commandment— obedience to the rest of God's will flows out of loving God and others.

14. The "Sam and Karen" scenario includes relational patterns from several couples. The names and details have been adapted for illustrative purposes.

15. Frederick Buechner, quoted by Mike and Danae Yankoski, *Zealous Love: A Practical Guide to Social Justice* (Grand Rapids: Zondervan, 2009), 53, says, "Not to love is, psychically, spiritually, to die. To live for yourself alone, hoarding your life for your own sake, is in almost every sense that matters to reduce your life to a life hardly worth the living, and thus to lose it."

16. One of the most intense forms of torture is the intentional deprivation of all physical sensations. The ones being tortured in such ways have been known to attempt serious self-inflicted injuries on themselves in an attempt to verify that they are still alive. Those whose emotions are numbed (for whatever reasons) will also engage in self-destructive behaviors, if for no other reason than to feel alive.

17. Our obsession with romantic love has led us to a place where we are becoming incapable of loving people in non-romantic relationships. I also fear that the end result of this will be the inability to love our spouses in committed, married relationships.

18. C. S. Lewis, *Mere Christianity* (New York: Macmillan Publishing Company, 1952), 116, 117.

19. Brennan Manning, *The Furious Longing of God* (Colorado Springs: David Cook, 2009), 85. In America we have allowed "cool cordiality and polite indifference" "to masquerade as the love of Jesus." A sad commentary on contemporary "rights" culture of today is that— whether from the left or right side of the political spectrum—love is not viewed as a sustainable way of life. The best thing the political world can offer is "let us try our best not to harass or kill each other," which is a far cry from Jesus' call to "love one another."

20. Scot McKnight, *The Jesus Creed: Loving God, Loving Others* (Brewster, MA: Paraclete Press, 2004), 57–58, says "Christians are not called to tolerance; Christians are called to love. Toleration condescends; love honors."

Chapter 3: In a World of Love

1. Two Hebrew words dominate the Old Testament references to love: *'ahab* and *hesed*. Depending on the context, these words can be used interchangeably. *'Ahab* means "to burn, kindle, or set on fire" and is used in reference to covenant love, but also friendship, familial, and romantic love. *Hesed* means "eagerness and ardent desire" and is the word often translated as "lovingkindness" or "steadfast love." The command to love God in Deuteronomy 6:5 and love one's neighbor in Leviticus 19:18 are both based on *'ahab*. The New Testament translates this as *agapeo*.

2. In Matthew 5:43–48, God's love is an expression of who He is, not as a result of who deserves His love. God blesses through loving actions to even people who are "evil" and "unjust." Love is who He is and therefore how He acts to all people. Jesus tells us that as His followers, we are to *be* love so that we *do* love in the same way God loves. Love is a part of the divine DNA. God acts loving because it is His nature to do so. Just as a corn plant can't act like a cat because it's not its nature to do so, neither can God act unloving because unlove is not in His nature. He can only act in a loving way because He *is* love.

3. A. W. Tozer, *The Radical Cross* (Camp Hill, PA: Wingspread Publishers, 2009), 126, says, "In everything that God does He acts like Himself." Brennan Manning, *The Furious Longing of God* (Colorado Springs: David Cook, 2009), 37–38, says:

    God is love is the fundamental meaning of the holy and adorable

Trinity. Put bluntly, God is sheer Being-in-Love and *there was never a time when God was not love*. The foundation of the furious longing of God is the Father who is the originating Lover, the Son who is the full self-expression of that Love, and the Spirit who is the original and inexhaustible activity of that Love.

See also Manning, *Furious Longing*, 62–63, for Catherine of Siena's discussion of how love is the fabric of the universe because of God's "drunk and crazy" love.

4. Love as one of the central character traits of God's nature interrelates to His other divine attributes. Love is the motivator behind God's justice, holiness, power, and goodness. Love even tempers His wrath with patience.

5. Wayne Grudem, *Systematic Theology: An Introduction to Biblical Doctrine* (Grand Rapids, MI: Zondervan, 1994), 198, says, "God's love means that God eternally gives of himself to others." Thomas Jay Oord, *Defining Love: A Philosophical, Scientific, and Theological Engagement* (Grand Rapids: Brazos Press, 2010), 19, says, "Love requires actual relations with others. Entirely isolated individuals, if such existed, could not love." Even within God, love cannot be expressed in a relationship vacuum.

6. Dallas Willard, *Renovation of the Heart: Putting on the Character of Christ* (Colorado Springs: NavPress, 2002), 184. Also see Jonathan Edwards, "Charity More Excellent than the Extraordinary Gifts of the Spirit," (www.reformedsermonarchives.com/edwardstitle.htm, sermon 26).

7. In John 17:24, Jesus said, "Father … you loved me before the foundation of the world." These words should give us pause to ponder that before there was anything created outside of God, He loved within Himself.

8. Psalm 136:4–9.

9. If you doubt me, just ask any biochemist, doctor, psychologist, or pastor. Better yet, get a group of them together and see if they can figure out why and how people do what they do. Humans are fascinatingly intricate with cells and systems interdependently relying upon other cells and systems. The mysteries of the human psyche have still never been unraveled after centuries of collective contemplation on our inner world. David sang it well when he said that we are "fearfully and wonderfully made" (Ps. 139:14).

10. Genesis 1:27.

11. Lewis, *Mere Christianity*, 65.

12. Genesis 2:18.
13. Robert Hemfelt, Frank Minirth, and Paul Meier, *Love Is a Choice: The Definitive Book on Letting Go of Unhealthy Relationships* (Nashville: Thomas Nelson, 1989), 27–28.
14. Quoted in John Ortberg, *Who Is This Man? The Unpredictable Impact of the Inescapable Jesus* (Grand Rapids, Zondervan: 2012), 153.
15. Evangelism that seriously affirms this fact will be more effective than those using more judgmental methods. Though most churches would deny or even blush at the fact that in bars and pubs around the world, friends can find a genuine care and concern for each other. Love through helpful actions is easily recognizable and readily accepted by people everywhere. Some of the best examples of love are not found in steepled churches, but in dark bars, dirty barns, military barracks, and over backyard fences.
16. More will be said about the importance of the body in expressing love in chapter 6.
17. God is love, but not all love is God. When we make our human definitions and experiences of love equal to God, then we create an idol.

Chapter 4: Incarnational Love

1. Incarnation comes from the Latin compound word *incarnare*, which means "to make flesh." The root word for flesh (*caro-, carnes-*) is still used in many Latin-based languages today. For example, in Spanish-speaking cultures, the butcher shop is referred to as *la carneceria*. Carnivorous refers to "meat or flesh eaters." Carnival is from the Old Latin, *carnelevare*, which means "to take away meat" (referring to Lent). As Mardi Gras (a.k.a.: Fat Tuesday) took on a festive atmosphere of last indulgences before Lent, the word carnival soon referred to the fleshly party instead of personal worship and sacrifice. But all these words are rooted in *carne*, meat or flesh.
2. John 14:9; Colossians 1:15; Hebrews 1:1–3. Peter L. Scazzero, *The Emotionally Healthy Church: A Strategy for Discipleship that Actually Changes Lives*, Updated and Expanded Edition (Grand Rapids: Zondervan, 2010), 180, 187–199. Scazzero sees three parts to Jesus' incarnation. First, Jesus entered our world. He adapted His life and ways to "fit in" here. Second, Jesus kept His identity. Jesus never questioned or forgot that He was God's Son from heaven. Third, He hung between the two realities of this world and heaven. He

maintained the tension between being fully here while being fully connected and engaged with His heavenly Father. Jesus the Word who was God and is God became flesh and lived among us.

3. The antichrists in 1 John denied that Jesus came in a physical body. Perhaps John's insistence on the physical embodiment of Jesus is less about Docetism or Gnostic dualism, but John's core conviction that Jesus demonstrated His love for the world and died for their sins with His physical body. Love must have a physical vehicle through which to be experienced; and those who deny this are antichrists.

4. "For God so loved the world, that he gave his only Son, that whoever believes in him should not perish but have eternal life. For God did not send his Son into the world to condemn the world, but in order that the world might be saved through him." John 3:16–17

5. See Matthew 3:17; 17:5; John 3:35; 5:20; 10:17; 15:9.

6. When Jesus gave evidence to the disciples of John the Baptist of His legitimacy as Messiah, He did not appeal to His feelings, thoughts, or intentions. Jesus listed specific loving actions in Luke 7:21–23—the blind receive sight, the lepers are cleansed, the lame walk, the dead are raised, the deaf hear, and the poor have the good news preached. The kingdom of God that Jesus preached was about loving *now*, not waiting only for the sweet by and by.

7. Henri Nouwen, *The Essential Henri Nouwen*, edited by Robert A. Jonas (Boston: Shambhala, 2009), 111, says: "Compassion is something other than pity. Pity suggests distance, even a certain condescension …. Compassion means to become close to the one who suffers. But we can come close to another person only when we are willing to become vulnerable ourselves." No one was more compassionate, and therefore as vulnerable, as Jesus.

8. Jesus' love was enormous in scope and beautifully nuanced, but it was never confused about what to do or presented as optional. He just loved God and people in a simple, uncomplicated way.

9. Mark 14:36.

10. In John 15:10, Jesus says, "If you keep my commandments, you will abide in my love, *just as I have kept my Father's commandments and abide in his love*" (emphasis added).

11. 1 John 3:5, "You know that he appeared to take away sin, and in him there is no sin." For there to be a substitutionary sacrifice offered for sin, a physical body was required. I believe this is behind 1 John's emphasis upon Jesus appearing in the flesh. The problem with

Docetism is that it fails to account for the reality of and need for the incarnation.

12. Romans 8:38–39; Romans 5:5.
13. 1 John 3:1.
14. 1 John 4:19

Chapter 5: Love Tank

1. At the conclusion of my hike, I consulted with a Park Ranger who said that due to the off-season, I was the only person known to be in the area at the time (estimated at over 200 square miles). How's that for solitude!
2. Chapman, *Five Love Languages*, 20, says, "Among … [a child's] emotional needs, none is more basic than the need for love and affection, the need to sense that he or she belongs and is wanted."
3. See John 4:4–43.
4. Manning, *Furious Longing*, 76, paraphrases Basil Hume.
5. Romans 5:5.
6. Here I'm focusing on what's involved for us to experience of His love, not "works" that we do to earn His love. God's love is given without conditions; it is experienced with conditions.
7. Bill Thrall, Bruce McNicol, and John Lynch, *TrueFaced: Trust God and Others with Who You Really Are* (Colorado Springs: NavPress, 2004), 86.
8. Augustine. http://thinkexist.com/quotes/saint_augustine/2.html. Charles H. Spurgeon, *12 Sermons on the Love of Christ*, "Love's Birth and Parentage," 4th Printing (Grand Rapids: Baker Books, 1993), 38, says, "But there is love in the heart of every true-born child of God; it is as needful to spiritual life as blood to the natural life."
9. Bill Thrall and Bruce McNicol, *The Kingdom Life: A Practical Theology of Discipleship and Spiritual Formation*, "Communities of Grace," edited by Alan Andrews (Colorado Springs: NavPress, 2010), 71.
10. Thrall and McNicol, *Kingdom Life*, 64.
11. Gary Gulbranson, quoted by Richard Stearns, *The Hole in Our Gospel* (Nashville: Thomas Nelson, 2009), 87.
12. Thrall and McNicol, *Kingdom Life*, 77.
13. Thrall, McNicol, and Lynch, *TrueFaced*, 92.
14. Ephesians 3:18–19.
15. McKnight, *Jesus Creed*, 107.
16. A great book on the nuts and bolts of practicing the daily presence

of God is Frank C. Laubach, *Letters by a Modern Mystic* (Colorado Springs: Purposeful Design Publications, 2007).

17. Willard, *Getting Love Right*; John Burke, *Soul Revolution: How Imperfect People Become All God Intended* (Grand Rapids: Zondervan, 2008), 52–53.

18. Stephen and Alex Kendrick, *The Love Dare* (Nashville: B&H Publishing, 2008), 141, says "When God is your reason for loving, your ability to love is guaranteed. That's because loves comes from Him."

19. Francis Chan, *Forgotten God: Reversing Our Tragic Neglect of the Holy Spirit* (Colorado Springs: David Cook, 2009), 96.

20. 2 Corinthians 12:15, Amplified Bible.

Chapter 6: The Art of Love

1. I am gratefully indebted to thinkers and writers who have critically engaged themselves in thinking through the deeper aspects of love, especially C.S. Lewis, Dallas Willard, and Thomas Oord.

2. C.S. Lewis' book, *The Four Loves*, (San Diego: Harvest Book, 1960), is a classic on this theme. He explains the nuances of the Greek words *storge* (affection), *eros* (romantic/erotic love), *philos* (friendship), and *agape* (charity).
   To refer to *agape* love as "Christian" does not mean that non-Christians cannot express sacrificial love. Jesus Himself says that godless people show *agape* (Matt. 6:46–47), but only in reciprocal relationships. The power of Jesus' understanding of *agape* is that it is to be extended out to all people, not just those who will return love. Jesus' explanation of love added a scope and depth that was unthinkable to both the religious elite and the pagan masses until His appearing.
   May, *Love: A History*, 21, notes that the rise of the importance of *agape* came with the translation of the Hebrew Scriptures into Greek (the Septuagint or LXX). Most of the Hebrew words for love were translated in the LXX as *agape*, "until then an infrequently used term." Jesus added content and context to the preexisting idea of *agape*.

3. 1 John 4:8, 16.

4. 1 John 4:19.

5. In John 15:11, the full joy that Jesus wants in us is the joy of experiencing His love and sharing His love with others.

6. Again, think in terms of the big picture vs. a flowchart. The order of the first three isn't as important as the need for them all to be present.

7. Matthew 14:14ff.

8. Luke 10:33–34.
9. See Matthew 11:28–30.
10. 1 John 5:3.
11. "Forced" love may still be of some benefit to the other person. For example, food is a fine thing to give the hungry person, even if you are reluctant and don't do it freely and graciously. But it's hard to call "forced" love *agape*; it's more akin to duty.
12. I use the picture of marriage with freedom because it is our highest level of love in "normal life." We enter into marriage freely and must stay there freely. As we learn to choose love as a free act of our wills, the same model is applied to others around us who are not our spouses.
13. McKnight, *Jesus Creed*, 207, "The disciplines of the Christian life are 'bodily acts of love' and cannot be set aside if we are being spiritually formed."

    I have questioned deeply why there is no spiritual discipline of love, like we promote the disciplines of prayer, fasting, silence, frugality, and so on. I believe that love should be included as a part of the great spiritual disciplines because it is the highest goal of the Christian life. The regular, daily pursuit of loving others intentionally and genuinely could only help us be more Christlike, right? Although I have yet to read or hear anyone speak specifically on this topic, my speculation is that love is seen by most as a fruit of the Spirit that cannot be practiced, but will show up in our lives as the result of Spirit-led living. I still believe there is a place to pursue love as a spiritual discipline nonetheless.
14. James 2:26.
15. Dallas Willard, *The Spirit of the Disciplines: Understanding How God Changes Lives* (New York: Harper One, 1991), 20.
16. Arthur A. Vogel, *Radical Christianity and the Flesh of Jesus* (Grand Rapids: William B. Eerdmans Publishing Company, 1995), 37.
17. 1 John 3:14–14; 4:20–21.
18. C.S. Lewis, *Mere Christianity* (New York: Macmillan Publishing Company, 1952), 115–117. Lewis focuses on love as an act of the will. Dallas Willard, *Getting Love Right*, focuses on loving being a disposition to love, but not a feeling. It's also worth noting that most Christian counselors and psychologists do not equate love with feelings, but with loving actions.
19. We don't love for personal improvement, but for the benefit we can give to others. As we extend ourselves unselfishly to others, we will change to be more like Christ.

Chapter 7: Swimming in Love

1. For those interested, I'd like to swim across the Mississippi River, the Chesapeake Bay, the Bosphorus River, the Suez Canal, the Panama Canal, and to Alcatraz and back. Recently, I bagged one of my long-term goals of jumping in the frigid waters of Loch Ness in Scotland.
2. In 1 Timothy 4:7–8, we are exhorted to train ourselves for godliness. We are not called to try to be godly, but to train to be godly. In the same way, we must train ourselves through intentional and repetitive actions to love, not try to love. The more we learn how to love, the more we'll have a "feel" for what is loving. Love may not become easy, as love often includes suffering (see chapter 8), but we can know that we are making forward progress in this area.
3. Len Schlesinger and Charles Kiefer, *Action Trumps Everything: Creating What You Want in an Uncertain World* (Duxbury, MA: Blank Ink Press, 2110).
4. Clare de Graaf, *The 10 Second Rule* (USA: Graaf, 2010), 39.
5. Seth Godin, *Poke the Box* (USA: Do You Zoom, Inc., 2011), 12.
6. John 14:15.
7. Gary Chapman, *The Five Love Languages: How to Express Heartfelt Commitment to Your Mate* (Chicago: Northfield Publishing, 1995). The five love languages Chapman proposes are: meaningful touch, quality time, acts of service, gifts, and words of encouragement.
8. Perhaps this phenomenon is not a problem with Chapman's method, but with the immature person who functionally is monolingual and bilingual at best. People who genuinely "speak" all five languages are incredibly rare.
9. To be clear, the "one another" passages are inspired; my categorization isn't. The focus is on showing love to others through obeying the commands of Christ, not creative organization of the commands.
10. Smalley and Trent, *Love Is a Decision*, 65.
11. Augustine was asked, "What does love look like?" His answer: "It has the hands to help others. It has feet to hasten to the poor and needy. It has eyes to see misery and want. It has ears to hear the sighs and sorrows of men. That is what love looks like." In essence, love cares about the needs of others. www.brainquotes.com/quotes/authors/s/saint-augustine_2.html.
12. John Ortberg, *The Life You've Always Wanted* (Grand Rapids: Zondervan, 1997), 87.
13. Ephesians 4:15.
14. 1 Corinthians 13:6.

15. See Matthew 23.
16. James 1:19.
17. According to 1 John 4:21–22, love for God requires that we love other people. In this sense, there is no privatization of love for God, meaning that we can't have the stance that "it's just God and me, stay out of my personal religion." If we love God, we must love all those people around us, however annoying they may be.
18. Willard, *Renovation of the Heart*, 183.
19. Willard, *Renovation of the Heart*, 183.
20. 1 John 4:12, 17, 18.

Chapter 8: Love Hurts

1. Romans 5:8.
2. Kyle Idleman, *Not a Fan: Becoming a Completely Committed Follower of Jesus* (Grand Rapids: Zondervan, 2011), 145, "A committed love is best demonstrated through sacrifice."
3. Persons of whatever religion or belief that use terrorism and/or suicide bombs are not martyrs to their faith. They are murderers. They seek to kill, not heal and give life. They are not acting for the good of others. Martyrs will die for their faith, but they won't kill for it. Martyrs are persecuted specifically for their faith and can find redemptive meaning in their suffering.
   Richard Wurmbrand, *Tortured for Christ* (Bartlesville, OK: Living Sacrifice Book Company, 1998), 38, says that it was love for Christ that enabled him to resist brainwashing and endure torture at the hands of the Soviet Communists. "Heart-washing" counters brainwashing.
4. The Greek words have been added in brackets to clarify the difference between *agapeo* (sacrificial love) and *phileo* (friendship love) that are indistinct with the single English word "love."
5. Mother Teresa, *No Greater Love*, 98, "To love, it is necessary to give. To give, it is necessary to be free from selfishness."
6. If parents waited for immediate reciprocity of love before caring for their children, the human race wouldn't last a generation.
7. At Deion Sanders' induction into the NFL Hall of Fame, he said "I always had a rule in life that I would never love anything that couldn't love me back." Although he was referring to football, this is the life philosophy for most. *Tulsa World*, 07 August 2011, B1.
8. See Matthew 5:43–48 and Luke 6:32–36. God loves all people in spite

of the fact that they do not love Him back. By our love without strings attached, we show ourselves to be His children.

9. Paula Fuller, "Participating in God's Mission," *Kingdom Life*, 213–214.

10. Matthew 5:46; Luke 6:32, 7:5.

11. I've also noticed a frequently repeated scenario where someone has an incredible love for people far away, for example orphans on the other side of the world, but they have little love for their actual husband, wife, children, or coworker.

12. The rich, young ruler walked away from Jesus without returning His love, yet Mark 10:21 says that Jesus loved him anyway.

13. Thomas Moore, Forward remarks in *No Greater Love*, ix.

14. Other excellent, but less known examples of love can be found in Dan Merchant, *Lord, Save Us from Your Followers* (Nashville: Thomas Nelson, 2008), 202. "It's one thing to write a check to your favorite charity; it's one thing to speak in sympathetic terms about the plight of those less fortunate; it's one thing to hand out blankets to homeless people; and it's *another* to get down on your hands and knees and lovingly wash the feet of a homeless person. To pour yourself into a simple act that says, 'I love you, you are special to me and to God.'"

15. Lewis, *Four Loves*, 169.

16. Matthew 5:38–42; 1 Corinthians 6:1–8. The real test for love is the capacity to love people who seek to ruin you. Anyone can love people who are nice and kind, but only a person filled with God's *agape* is able to love those who are evil and mean.

    I am not suggesting that persons in abusive situations simply passively take the abuse hurled at them by abusers. Abuse should always be limited and eliminated, when and as it is possible. On the other hand, love, even toward abusers, should not be limited. Love never stops acting for the good of others because love has become *who* we are as Christ-followers, and love is not withheld from people we may think don't deserve it.

17. 1 Thessalonians 3:12. We are called to love all people, not just other believers. While the limitations of our physical bodies keep us from being able to personally love each individual person in the world, we are to love all the ones within our sphere of influence.

18. John 13:35, 15:8.

19. John 13:34, 15:9, 12.

20. Thomas Merton, quoted by John Ortberg, "Don't Waste a Crisis," *Leadership Journal*: Winter, 2011, 39–40: "As long as we are on earth, the

love that unites us will bring us suffering by our very contact with one another, because this love is the resetting of a Body of broken bones."

Chapter 9: The Love Test

1. The *Left Behind* series is a sixteen book Christian bestseller written by Tim LaHaye and Jerry B. Jenkins about the end of the world. Published from 1995-2007 by Tyndale House.
2. Acts 16:31; Romans 3:28; Ephesians 2:8–9; and many other such passages clearly teach that salvation comes through faith in Christ alone. I am not decreasing the value of faith, but am seeking to increase the value of love.
3. It's worth noting that in Romans 5:1–5 and 2 Peter 1:5–7 faith is the starting point of our relationship with God, and *agape* is the final goal. The same overall emphasis is in the book of Ephesians, which begins with salvation by grace through faith in Christ and crescendos into walking in love as Christ loved us.
4. 1 Corinthians 13:7–8a. Wurmbrand, 39, says "God will judge us not according to how much [suffering] we endured, but how much we could love."
5. Mother Teresa, *No Greater Love*, 140, "At the moment of death, we will not be judged by the amount of work we have done but by the weight of love we have put into our works [of charity]. This love should flow from self-sacrifice, and it must be felt to the point of hurting."
6. In Matthew 7:21–23, Jesus says:

    "Not everyone who says to me, 'Lord, Lord,' will enter the kingdom of heaven, but the one who does the will of my Father who is in heaven. On that day many will say to me, 'Lord, Lord, did we not prophesy in your name, and cast out demons in your name, and do many mighty works in your name?' And then will I declare to them, 'I never knew you; depart from me, you workers of lawlessness.'"

    The key to interpreting this passage (as well as Matthew 7:24–27 that follows) is love. The ones who *do* the Father's will are safe; they add love and relational intimacy to their activities. Those who use the right words and perform amazing feats of ministry apart from love are rejected as unknown. True disciples are lovers of God and others; they and can be assured of their entry into the kingdom. Unlovers, however outwardly spiritual they may appear, will be shocked at their non-admission into the kingdom.

7. Mother Teresa, *No Greater Love*, 59.

8. Louise Beal summarizes the Golden Rule of the goats: "Love thy neighbor as thyself, but choose your neighborhood" (quote in *Tulsa World*, January 14, 2012). Sadly, this is precisely what most Christians do.

9. Mother Teresa, *No Greater Love*, 22, "Do not think that love, in order to be genuine, has to be extraordinary." Also see 1 John 5:20–21.

Chapter 10: The Love People

1. Sister sites are located on their homepage and include: www. GodHatesIslam.com; www.GodHatesTheMedia.com; www. GodHatesTheWorld.com; and www.AmericaIsDoomed.com. The Westboro Baptist Church not only promotes its own version of hate, but supports other hate-groups.

2. Institutionalized hate is also found in many groups, not just churches: such as White Supremacy groups, radical feminist groups, radical Muslim groups, and radical liberation-theology groups. I believe that these groups rally their members around hate for hate's ability to clearly identify a common foe. Hate unifies and distinguishes them from their enemies, but it does not provide them with any pathway to positively impact the world around them.

3. The issue of hell can be addressed as God's method for dealing with people who do not want His love. If someone ultimately chooses to reject God's love, God chooses to honor their choice with a dreadful place completely devoid of love (i.e., hell). The Greek word *Gehenna* refers to the cosmic dump for the irretrievably useless (Willard, *Renovation*, 55–58). Loveless people are of no value to the kingdom of God. People are not arbitrarily sent to hell because they are bad (we're all sinful), but because they have rejected the love and life of God offered in Christ. For people who reject God's love, an eternity of heaven—where God's love saturates the whole environment—would be hell. The person who does not enjoy God's love will find heaven tedious and unfulfilling. The loving God takes no delight in people going to hell, but makes provision for them, since love must always been chosen, not forced.

4. James 3:10.

5. Palmer Chinchen, *Waiting for Daylight: God's Hope for Dark Nights* (Chandler, AZ: Movement Publishing, 2007), "Evangelicals have a poor reputation for love … we're not known for living love." Merchant, *Lord,*

Save Us, 36, says that when the adjectives of born-again or evangelical are added to the word Christian, most Americans think you are "a Republican who hates gays, abortionists, and the ACLU." Merchant, 187–188, also says that "people are tired of hearing about love and *not* seeing enough of us show it. It's time to *do*."

6.   Brian McLaren, *A Generous Orthodoxy*, (Grand Rapids: Zondervan, 2004), 249, "Because we follow Jesus, because Jesus moves toward all people in love and kindness and grace, *we do the same.* Our Christian identity must not make us afraid of, superior to, isolated from, defensive or aggressive toward, or otherwise hostile to people of other religions. Rather, the reverse."

7.   St. Aristides the Philosopher of Athens, *The Apology of Aristides the Philosopher*, Translated by D.M. Kay, www.earlychristianwritings.com/text/aristides-kay.html.

8.   www.earlychurch.com/unconditional-love.php.

9.   Christine Caine, "Leading on the Edge of Hope," Global Leadership Summit, August 5, 2110.

10.   Proverbs 4:23.

11.   The phrase translated as "you have abandoned the love you had at first" (Rev. 2:4) can be legitimately interpreted two ways according to the original Greek language: "you have left your first love" (i.e., God) or "you abandoned the love you had at first" (i.e., love for God and others). Since nothing in the context specifically limits this abandonment to God alone and since the repentance commanded includes "works," I believe that this is an indictment of the overall love of the Ephesians and not merely their love toward God. Love for God *and* others must be rekindled through repentance and loving actions.

12.   Scazzero, 199, says that when incarnational love is the church's priority, the definition of success changes from simply "doing more, 'fixing' people, or arranging the world into something we consider God-glorifying." Scazzero, 180, also says "The indispensable mark of spiritual maturity is not about recognition, numbers, spiritual gifts, or biblical knowledge. The essence of a genuine spiritual life is to love—God, ourselves, and other people." Love is the motivation and foundation for all service, ministry, giving, evangelism, or spiritual habits.

13.   Manning, *Furious Longing*, 89.

14.   1 John 3:14.

15.   More often than money or "charity," marginalized people crave acknowledgement. To acknowledge a person requires our presence and

undivided attention. Most of us would rather write a check or be an automaton in a soup kitchen.

16.   Mother Teresa, *No Greater Love*, 12.

Do Love Together: Project Ideas

1.   *Extreme Makeover: Home Edition* was an ABC reality television program that had a team of volunteers renovate a home for a needy family. It ran from 2003-2012.

Do Love Together

Project Ideas

Do Love encourages local churches and small groups to demonstrate love tangibly to others. An endless variety of ways can be created and implemented. The following ideas are ones that have been used effectively at my home fellowship, Freedom Church, in a single year. Freedom is *not* a mega church, so know that you don't have to be large to be loving and effective.

- Organize a food drive and provide pick-up/delivery for a local food bank.
- Find families through the food bank that may need yard care, house cleaning, or small repairs and send a team of volunteers out to help them on a Saturday.
- Sanitize a local gym and the equipment there for a gymnastic organization for under-resourced families.
- Collect and deliver gently used furniture and appliances to international students at local universities.
- Collect and deliver diapers, wipes, and other supplies for mothers and babies to a local pregnancy resource center.
- Make baby blankets for a pregnancy resource center.
- Roast ears of fresh corn and give it away at a city-sponsored fall festival.
- Host a community-wide block party for the Fourth of July. Give away hamburgers, hotdogs, and trimmings. Provide inflatables, games, live music, fireworks, and fun for the whole family.
- Renovate a home (think *Extreme Makeover: Home Edition*)[1] for a local charity that serves under-resourced people.

- Host a Thanksgiving banquet for children in DHS foster care (who do not have adoptive parents).
- Collect and ship used cell phones and laptop computers to new business people in a developing nation (Kenya).
- Provide money for backpacks filled with school supplies and small toys for children in Mexico.
- Provide coffee, cookies, and popcorn for two precincts that serve thousands of voters during the national election.

DO LOVE

Leader's Note: If you are using this study guide as a group leader, please refer to biblical references in the endnotes of each chapter. The purpose of this study guide is to facilitate discussion *with the goal of encouraging people to actually do love.*

Also, have participants sign up for at least one week in which each will write out his or her own "Confession of a Love Hack." Direct group members to be real and to focus on their own love hack moments (not someone else's). Have them read aloud their "Confessions" to the group. If time allows, have them do this exercise more than once. This honest admission of failure is not only healthy, but crucial to growing in Christlike love.

Introduction and Chapter 1: Love Hack

Read 1 Corinthians 13:1–8.

1. Why is love such an important topic?

2. What does the author mean by "unlove," and do you agree with his assessment?

3. Do you think of yourself as a love hack? Why or why not?

4. How has the simple definition of love as "patient and kind" (1 Cor. 13:4) been expressed through you in the past week? How have you struggled with being patient and kind?

5. In John 13:34, Jesus says to "love one another as I have loved you." Briefly share how Christ has loved you.

6. In what ways do you think God wants to change your understanding of love? How will this new understanding be expressed through your actions?

7. List the four stages of the Love Flywheel.
   1)
   2)
   3)
   4)

   On which stage do you find yourself most often? Why do you think this is?

   What will it take for you to go to the next stage (or to repeat the process)?

Chapter 2: Love Sick

Read Luke 10:25–37.

1. Define love in one sentence.

2. Why is love such an important truth in the Bible?

3. Why do you think that Jesus focuses on love as the basis for the Great Commandment?

    > "'Which commandment is the most important of all?' Jesus answered, 'The most important is, "Hear, O Israel: The Lord our God, the Lord is one. And you shall love the Lord your God with all your heart and with all your soul and with all your mind and with all your strength."' The second is this: "You shall love your neighbor as yourself."' There is no other commandment greater than these." (Mark 12:28b–31)

4. In what way does unlove most often express itself in your relationships—assault or withdrawal?

5. Though understandably a sensitive subject, have you ever been the giver/recipient of abuse or neglect? Briefly explain your answer.

6. Why do you think that the people of our culture have equated love with "feelings" or "tolerance?"

7. Share a time when you have personally "loved short."

Chapter 3: In a World of Love

Read Romans 5:1-8.

1. In your own words, explain the meaning of the biblical phrase, "God is love."

2. Based on what you know about creation account in Genesis 1–2 and the incarnation of Jesus, what is the significance of humans being "embodied" as it relates to love?

3. Do you agree or disagree with the statement: "Love is no secret virtue of Christians, but it is God's gift to the world"? Explain your answer.

4. What does it mean for you to realize that love requires a body through which to express itself?

5. How does John 3:16 become the model for you to express love to others?

Chapter 4: Incarnational Love

Read John 1:1–14.

1. What does the word *incarnation* mean?

2. What is the significance of Jesus' earthly body as it relates to God's expression of love?

3. The greatest act of love in the history of the world was the death of Jesus Christ. How does His death express God's love to you personally?

4. Paraphrase 1 John 4:9–10, and then share it with someone else.

5. How does the resurrection of Jesus express God's love for you?

Chapter 5: Love Tank

Read John 4:1–15.

1. Describe a time in your life when you were spiritually thirsty. What led to this condition? What, if anything, has quenched your thirst?

2. On a scale of 1 (extremely hard) to 10 (very easy), how easy/hard is it for you to *experience* (not merely know about) the love of God expressed through Jesus?

3. Four steps are given that position you under the "love spout of God." List the four steps below.
    1)
    2)
    3)
    4)

    Where are you in this process?

4. How full/empty is your personal love tank? How does this influence how you love others?

5. According to Psalm 81:10b, what is your responsibility and what is God's?

6. What is the best way(s) for you personally to keep your love tank filled?

Chapter 6: The Art of Love

Read 1 John 4:7–11.

1. Do you tend to explain love more as an engineer or as an art docent? Why?

2. What do you see are the similarities and differences between Christian love (*agape*) and …

   1) Affectionate or familial love—

   2) Romantic or erotic love—

   3) Friendship love—

3. What makes Christian love (*agape*) unique?

4. What does it mean to say that "love can be expressed without being reciprocated, but it cannot be experienced unless embraced"?

5. List the five "colors" involved in a single act of love.

    1)

    2)

    3)

    4)

    5)

    Which one is easiest for you? Which one is most difficult?

6. What is your response to the statement that "we are never commanded in Scripture to '*feel* love for another,' but simply to *do love*"?

Chapter 7: Swimming in Love

Read Romans 12:9–21.

1. Several things in life cannot be learned merely through obtaining an intellectual knowledge of them—swimming, playing an instrument, riding a bicycle, etc. A certain physical "feel" is learned in the process of doing the activity. The author says, "Love is learned in the act of doing it." What does this really mean for loving God and others?

2. Explain the phrase: "Inaction equals unlove."

3. What most often keeps you from acting *immediately* in a loving way?

4. List the seven categories of love based on the thirty-seven "one another" passages.

   1)

   2)

   3)

   4)

   5)

   6)

   7)

5. Of the seven categories of ways of loving one another, which one

   —is easiest for you to do?

   —is most difficult for you to do?

   —surprised you by being on the list?

   —do you think is most neglected?

6. If you were to ask a family member or a close friend, which "one-anothers" would they say are seen most clearly through your actions? Which ones would they say are infrequent or noticeably missing?

7. What is meant by the idea of "perfect love" (Matthew 5:48 and 1 John 4:12, 17, 18)?

Chapter 8: Love Hurts

Read Matthew 5:43–48.

1. The passion and death of Jesus Christ clarified that God's *agape* for us did not come without painful sacrifice. Read the following passages and reflect on the suffering that Jesus endured for us because of His love.

    Psalm 22:1, 6–8, 14–18.

    Isaiah 52:14; 53:2–8.

    Matthew 27:27–44.

2. How would you answer Jesus if He were to ask you directly, "Do you really love (*agapeo*) Me?"

3. What was your original motivation for following Jesus? Has that motivation changed as you've grown closer to Him; and if so, how?

4. Why do you believe that people expect love to be reciprocally expressed? How hard is it for you to express love without expecting or demanding a reciprocal response?

5. What is the riskiest part of love for you personally? What do you fear most?

6. How does love absorb hate and evil? What sustains love during these personal attacks?

7. At the close of the chapter, three simple truths are given about love. List these, and tell which one spoke to you personally.

    1)

    2)

    3)

Chapter 9: The Love Test

Read Matthew 25:31–46.

1. If love (and love alone) for God and others was the sole criterion by which your life would be evaluated before the judgment seat, how might this change the way that you live now?

2. Why do you think that love so easily becomes eclipsed in the lives of believers today?

3. Write out your thoughts on the haunting phrase of Jesus that describes the deterioration of love in the last days. He says, "The love of many will grow cold" (Matt. 24:12). Share this with the group.

4. What are some practical steps you can take to prevent this cooling of love from happening in your life?

5. In the parable of the sheep and the goats (Matt. 25:31–46), list out the loving activities that the sheep did and that the goats did not do.

6. What is the reason why the sheep did loving actions while the goats didn't?

7. Mother Teresa describes the marginalized people of this world as Jesus "in His distressing disguise." Who are these people in your life? Name them.

8. How might you tangibly demonstrate love this week to Jesus "in His distressing disguise?"

Chapter 10: The Love People

Read John 13:34–35.

1. What kinds of people do you find it most difficult to love? Why?

2. Why do you believe that Christians (as a whole) are not known as "the love people" of Jesus?

3. Do you believe the assessment by unbelievers that Christians are hypocritical is accurate? Why or why not?

4. What is your response to the "back in the day" testimonies regarding the early church's love for each other?

5. In Revelation 2:2–5, Jesus gave an evaluation of the church at Ephesus. His primary accusation was that "you have abandoned the love you had at first." Jesus then says to "repent and do the works you did at first." Explain repenting from unlove.

6. What are the works of love you need to immediately start as a result of this study?

7. What loving activity could your church do (as a group) that would express love to your community?

8. How has *Do Love* changed your understanding of love? How has it changed your expression of love in everyday life?

Special Thanks

Thanks ... Grazie ... Danke ... Merci ... Gracias ... Xie xie ... Asante sana ... Shukran ... Dhanyevaad

While it may be true that writing is a solitary exercise of an afflicted soul, editing is a group project where the writer inflicts his work on others. Several people provided excellent feedback and editing recommendations for this book. They include: Trenna Bingham, Paul Taylor, Cole Hedgecock, Scott Hamilton, Talon Noh, and Randy and Regina Gill. Special thanks go to Megan Moore for her additional help in reading, editing, researching, and encouraging me throughout the whole project. I am also grateful to the editorial and design teams at WestBow Press for their professional assistance in preparing this book for publication.

I am indebted to Dr. Adrian Alexander and the staff of the McFarland Library at the University of Tulsa for graciously providing me a quiet place to study and write. Their technical assistance, research expertise, and administrative help greatly aided me in maximizing my limited sabbatical break.

Without the generous sabbatical grant from the Lilly Foundation that provided both uninterrupted time and financial resources for this project, it is doubtful that *Do Love* would have come into fruition. Their consistent concern for pastoral renewal is love in action on a mass scale.

Freedom Church in Owasso, Oklahoma has been incredibly patient and gracious to me in allowing me to take the time to write. They have been instrumental in teaching me how to love; their enthusiasm for "doing love together" has benefited thousands of people. They have helped me refine my thoughts on love through sermons, daily examples, and private conversations. Thank you for loving me.

To my three sons: thanks for your support and encouragement. Your adventurous spirits and love for God always call me onward and upward. I'm proud of the men you are becoming.

My wife, Laurie, has been the one through whom God has most clearly, consistently, and powerfully taught me about love. She has patiently put up with my love hacking for over twenty-five years of marriage. Thanks for "doing me good and not evil" all the days of my life. You are God's gift of love to me.